THE
COMEBACK

GARY SHAPIRO

BEAUFORT
BOOKS

Excerpts from "Canada Lawmakers Ratify Free Trade Agreement With Colombia, Send to Senate" by Theophilios Argitis. Used with permission of Bloomberg.com Copyright ©2010. All rights reserved.

Excerpts from "Colombia: Exports to Reach $40 Billion '10; Double in 4 Years" by Darcy Crowe. Reprinted by permission of the *Wall Street Journal*, Copyright © 2010 Dow Jones & Company, Inc. All Rights Reserved Worldwide. License number 2550840759663.

Excerpts from "Two L.A. agencies get $111 million in stimulus funds but have created only 55 jobs" by David Zahniser. *Los Angeles Times*, Copyright ©2010. Reprinted with Permission. All rights reserved.

FIRST EDITION

Library of Congress Cataloging-in-Publication Data

Shapiro, Gary.
   The comeback : how innovation will restore the American dream / Gary Shapiro.
      p. cm.
   ISBN 978-0-8253-0562-7 (alk. paper)
   1. Technological innovations—United States. 2. Entrepreneurship—United States. 3. American Dream. I. Title.
   HC110.T4S52 2011
   338'.0640973—dc22

                                    2010047997

For inquiries about volume orders, please contact:

Beaufort Books
27 West 20th Street, Suite 1102
New York, NY 10011
sales@beaufortbooks.com

Published in the United States by Beaufort Books
www.beaufortbooks.com

Distributed by Midpoint Trade Books
www.midpointtrade.com

Printed in the United States of America

10 9 8 7 6 5 4 3 2 1

To my wife Susan and to her parents, my grandparents, and every other American (including those no longer alive) who sacrificed so much to come to the United States. You left behind family, you had to learn a new language, you worked hard and sacrificed so much for your children. You have contributed to our economy, you are amazing citizens and huge patriots, and you have made the United States a beautiful and successful mosaic. We can repay our debt to you by ensuring the American Dream stays alive.

Contents

Foreword

I WAS ONCE asked to provide some advice to a company that at one point had a product that was not only the best in its class, but also technically far ahead of its competition. It created a better way of offering its service, and customers loved it and paid for it.

Then it made a fatal mistake.

It asked its customers what features they wanted to see in the product and then delivered on those features. It seemed like good business: Ask your customers what they want, and then give it to them.

Unfortunately for this company, its competitor didn't ask its customers what they wanted. Instead, the competitor had a vision of doing things differently. As a result, they did it better. Their customers didn't really see the value or need for those features until they saw the product. When they tried it, they loved it.

So what did the company I was working with do when it saw what the competition was doing, despite my admonitions to do otherwise? It repeated its mistake and once again asked its customers what they wanted in the product. Of course the customers responded with features that they now loved from the competitor, while the competitor continued to innovate.

The paradigm had shifted. Innovation had paved the way. The company I was advising? I made them memorize what Alan Kay once said: "The best way to predict the future is to invent it."

Consumers aren't sages. They aren't in the business of imagining the next great thing. That's the job of innovators, who don't have a choice. To borrow a phrase from my friend, Gary Shapiro, they either "innovate or die." Those who rely on someone else to tell them what the future holds usually find themselves six feet under before they even realize they're in the coffin.

But progress—real progress—is like that. It's punishing and it's merciless.

It's also absolutely vital for the continued prosperity of the United States. As Shapiro makes abundantly clear in the pages that follow, innovation is America's economic salvation. It creates wealth, jobs, even entire industries where nothing existed before. And innovation is the key in reversing our decline.

Like that company I worked with, our government is making a fatal mistake. It believes it is acting like a good business when it treats our economy like a focus group, asking each member of the group what it likes and what it doesn't like. Taking these answers, it then attempts to fashion our economic policy.

The results of this "innovation by committee" are plain for all to see: exploding deficits, minimal growth, anemic job creation, and an ever-growing reliance on government aid. Whether under Republican or Democratic administrations or Congresses, the United States has been mired in uncertainty for years.

This book is about how to reverse this process and restart America's innovation engine. It's about how to get America back on track and reassert our preeminence in the world.

I have had the privilege of knowing Gary Shapiro for many years. He has been at the forefront of protecting America's innovators since he helped beat back an attempt by the content community to bury the VCR thirty years ago. That was a defining moment for Shapiro, as it would be for the revolution in consumer electronics that followed. It was a fight that showed that the success or failure of innovation has as much to do with the effort to defend it as it does with the usefulness of the product.

I also worked closely with Shapiro as he helped lead the national transition to digital television. That successful effort disrupted the status quo but changed our nation for the better. Of course, along with thousands of others, I have also been to International CES, where innovation and the future are on display.

The result of those thirty years Shapiro has spent in the trenches, fighting for innovation, has led to the ideas presented here. This book is a policy guide for our lawmakers to follow if they are serious about fully enabling America's unique culture of entrepreneurship. He presents a disturbing picture of our current situation, and offers the tough choices we'll need to make to get ourselves out of it.

You probably won't agree with every one of his ideas. Whether you're a Republican or a Democrat, conservative or liberal, there's going to be something in this book that will challenge your long-held beliefs. Let it. It's time we stop focusing on the success of one party or ideology, and start focusing on the success of our country.

But this book is more than a policy memo, too. It is a plea from one American to another to remember the American Dream—the Dream that the author has lived, the Dream that I have been fortunate to live. The Dream our ancestors came to this country to live.

Mark Cuban
October 2010

Preface

My DEFINING MOMENT occurred In July 2008 at a lavish hotel in Qingdao, China. At a formal banquet I sat next to the head of the province, the top Communist presiding over some 100 million Chinese. With fewer than ten words, he changed me. In a few brief seconds, he planted a seed. This seed I received uneasily. In fact, for a while I just used it as an amusing anecdote. But the seed expanded, changed, and grew into a tree of resolve. This annoying man catalyzed my grief, denial, thought, and action—but never my acceptance.

I sat next to him as part of the formal opening banquet for the SINOCES, a trade show held each year in the beautiful coastal city of Qingdao. Little did I know, this event had started several years earlier and had borrowed part of the name from the International Consumer Electronics Show (CES). At the Consumer Electronics Association, CES is our pride and joy. It is the world's largest and most exciting homage to consumer technology innovation. Held each January in Las Vegas, with more than 2,500 companies exhibiting cool new stuff, International CES attracts more than 125,000 leaders from business, media, and government from around the world.

Based in Arlington, Virginia, the Consumer Electronics Association (CEA) is a nonprofit trade association of some 2,000 American companies who make and sell technology products. I have worked for or at CEA since I was a law student in 1979. Throughout my time here, I have been a part of every innovation, from the VCR and the PC to the CD to the Internet. By producing our CES trade show and guiding our government policy to foster and encourage innovation, I have had a front row seat in witnessing a technology innovation revolution. I have been privileged to see innovations that have changed the world, created millions of new jobs, and transformed how we receive information, entertainment, and education.

It has not always been easy. Technology innovation has also changed other industries, and not in pleasant ways. Innovation breeds progress, but it also destroys. Ask a typewriter mechanic if he has a lot of clients these days. We have fought many fights, but for the most part, we won the battles that would have restricted progress, and the world is now better. I am extremely proud that we have improved the world through innovative technology.

I anticipate each year's International CES like a kid entering a toy store. Nothing is more exciting than the new innovations and technologies and seeing how each of 2,500 companies position themselves to buyers, the media, investors, and the important executives. So as the CEO of the organization owning the CES name, I knew we had to act when we learned the CES name was being used in China with "SINOCES" without our permission.

SINOCES was created in 2001 by the electronics trade association in China and the city of Qingdao (famous for the Tsingdao beer). I knew a lawsuit in China was impractical, so we cut a deal. As both the city of Qingdao and our Chinese sister association shared our desire to create a big technology event for Asia, we negotiated a partnership through which we licensed our name, received a cut of the revenue, and helped with marketing, programs, speakers, and attendees. We also brought an American delegation, of which I was a member. It was a nice relationship—at least until 2008, when the economy softened.

Before the fall, the Chinese would do anything for us—even at the expense of their citizens. For example, in 2005, my wife Susan and I arrived in Beijing late, missing our connecting flight to Qingdao. The next few flights to Qingdao were full, so we told our partners we would not arrive until the next day. They said to stay put in the Beijing Airport. Within ten minutes, an official found us and whisked us to the Qingdao-bound plane waiting to take off on the tarmac. Two Chinese citizens had "voluntarily" given up their seats to accommodate us. Indeed, the Chinese did everything possible to give us an amazing experience, including police escorts and many celebratory meals.

Of course this graciousness is the result of a government that is a bit less democratic than ours. I knew those two Chinese passengers would not have given up their seats if we were in America. And for this reason I accepted the Chinese government's hospitality with a grain of salt.

But in 2008, things changed. For one, in April, Susan and I had a baby. Our healthy baby, Mark, was a delightful surprise, especially thrilling my wife's parents. My wife was an only child, and her immigrant parents by then were not expecting any grandchildren. I had two adult children from a prior marriage, but this miracle child later in life challenged me to think about the future—in particular, I wondered what kind of future he would have, knowing I probably would not be around for most of his life.

In 2008, the American economy also spiraled downward as the reality of the sub-prime mortgage debacle unfolded. It not only began a series of events affecting millions of Americans and Wall Street, but, as I learned, it also affected the Chinese and how they viewed the United States.

At the July 2008 event, from the moment I arrived in Qingdao, I was responding to questions about the American economy from our hosts and the Chinese press. At each protocol meeting, I was pressed by the Chinese on the issue of American sub-prime mortgages. They made it clear how unhappy they were with Americans, and they blamed our sub-prime mortgage problems on their reduced growth and sales. Clearly, they had ambitious growth goals, and jobs were on the line.

We had "protocol" meetings where I would sit in a big white chair next to an important Chinese government official or company executive. We would be separated by a coffee table with a huge bouquet of fragrant flowers, and behind us would sit two interpreters, one for each of us. Lined up in chairs by status and seniority on each side were our respective delegations, who had to feign interest as we talked in the time-consuming process of sequential English-to-Chinese and Chinese-to-English translations. Each meeting would begin with the sipping of the hot tea served by hostesses selected for the honor based on beauty and English proficiency. After the niceties, I would introduce our delegation, which included several American business executives interested in selling to or buying from the Chinese.

The final protocol meeting of the day was with a top Communist government leader. Although he was speaking Chinese, when I heard "sub-prime mortgage" I knew where he was heading. As protocol dictates, I listened intently. Despite my outward head-shaking and focus, inwardly I was constructing a different answer than I had been giving earlier. Previously I had responded to the sub-prime mortgage issue by saying that the American economy is the strongest in the world, that this is a minor blip and we will get through this and emerge stronger. I also insisted that the important thing is that trade between our two nations be bilateral. I raised issues of U.S. concern, including unbalanced trade, the environment, working conditions, piracy of intellectual property, restrictions on American exports to China, and the value of the Chinese currency.

But I decided to try a different approach in this final meeting. I told the Chinese government official I had good news. I turned to the American delegation and said that I understood his concerns about sub-prime mortgages. I then informed him that not one American in our delegation had a sub-prime mortgage. You could tell by their heartfelt laughter which Chinese official understood English. That deflected the situation immediately, at least for the couple of hours before the opening banquet and my transformational interaction with the senior Communist Chinese official.

The banquet began with speeches and toasts, and I was seated next to the head of the entire province. This Communist official seemed particularly grumpy and, in an earlier protocol meeting, had berated me for the U.S. sub-prime problems. As he was the top Chinese official and I was the top American, we were seated in the center of the VIP table with interpreters seated behind us. The speeches had ended, the entertainers had not yet taken the stage, and a moment for conversation had begun. And that's when it happened.

He turned to me and pointed his thumb up in the air. "China going up," he said in English. I nodded.

He then turned his thumb down and moved his hand toward the floor. "U.S. going down," he declared.

I was stunned. I did not immediately respond. I felt my blood boiling. In fact, I wanted to punch him.

I pulled my chair back, excused myself, and walked over to one of my board members, Henry Chiarelli, a wonderful Italian American and former Radio Shack executive. Henry calmed me down, and we shared some choice words about this repugnant idiot.

Every day since then, I have thought about that brief exchange. For a while, I chided myself for not having some immediate comeback. I could have responded by putting my thumb on the floor and showing China's rise one inch and then standing on my chair and showing the United States going down one inch. Or I could have simply slugged him and suffered the consequences.

But a couple of weeks later in Chicago at a CEA meeting, Henry was kind enough to describe my actions to his board colleagues as diplomacy under fire. That recognition—that I should not be angry at myself or even care what some coarse Communist official said—transformed my views. My anger over this Chinese insult transformed into a horrible conclusion. It is not that China was going up—that is a fact. Good for them.

Rather, it is the corollary fact: America *is* going down. The truth can hurt.

This appears so harsh in print. It is unfashionable to acknowledge and, some would argue, unpatriotic to declare the decline of one's country. Politicians don't get elected and business leaders don't succeed and books don't sell by declaring that America is faltering. Such a statement defies our culture of optimism and the sense of greatness that defines America.

But Americans are not stupid, and when presented with the facts, we can deal with them.

The fact of the decline is unmistakable. It stems from our choking debt and is exacerbated by government actions making the situation worse. The sub-prime mortgage debacle of 2008 was our clarion call.

I am as responsible as anyone. I knew about it. I certainly could have done more. I warned about it in our association magazine; I spoke about it when I gave speeches. In a 2007 meeting, I urged a Federal Trade Commissioner to focus on sub-prime mortgages when he summoned me to his office, concerned that Americans did not fully understand the transition to digital television.

Indeed, in 2007 and 2008, when consumer group and government leaders were concerned about the transition to digital television, I was consistent in raising the issue. I would say—even as head of the world's largest consumer electronics trade association—that losing television service for a few days is of minor importance compared to the fact that millions of Americans would lose their homes because they did not understand the mortgage documents they had signed.

In retrospect, I should have shouted louder. After all, what is more important to the innovation industry than the overall health of the U.S. economy? Or, more crassly, we sell fewer new products and services to nations with struggling economies. And years later, our economy is still struggling from the impact of the sub-prime crisis. In retrospect, what issue was more important than the harsh impact of sub-prime mortgages on the U.S. economy?

I still keep wondering why I have heard not one person in any position of responsibility actually take responsibility. How is it that we faced an easily foreseeable crisis and no one is responsible? What about the executives who headed the mortgage lenders like Countrywide and Washington Mutual? Other than some minor civil fines, they are living nicely thanks to their ill-gotten gains. What about the political leaders who rejected Bush Administration pleas to reform the promiscuous lending entities? Some are still ensconced in Congress and congratulating themselves for passing the 2010 financial "reform" legislation.

What about the Clinton and Bush Administration regulators who did not do their jobs and review these schemes for fraud and ascertain that mortgage applications were being checked and verified? What of the consumer groups advocating for housing ownership by the poor and greater equality of income? They are still encouraging laws that put lower-class Americans in a precarious financial position.

What of the bond-rating agencies who packaged the sub-prime mortgages and rated them safe? Author Michael Lewis in *The Big Short* describes how these agencies relied on borrower credit scores and cleverly included lending to recent immigrants (with no bad credit history and thus high scores) to give high average scores and thus high ratings to sub-prime notes. Yet these agencies and their executives continue to prosper.

What of the investigative journalists who missed this obvious story?

Housing mortgages don't have much to do with innovation. But the story from beginning to end, when it ends, revealed that our government is wildly ill-suited to manage our economy. Our government's response to the sub-prime mortgage disaster underscores a blinding incompetence that is hard to fathom. The response was but the latest in a multitude of foolish mistakes that have crippled America's number one brand: innovation. That Chinese Communist was correct. And unless we accept that, we will never return to our once-unconquerable heights.

My dream is to return to China in ten years and meet with him again. Behind me, I want a strong U.S. economy, building markets and expanding humanity's technological progress. I want him to envy America, rather than look down his nose at us. I want to return to that Chinese man and extend my thumb, pointing upward.

1

America's Decline

A TALE OF TWO CITIES

Almost every week, I experience a tale of two cities as I travel from Washington, D.C., to Detroit to see my wife and toddler son. For Washington, it is the best of times. Today's U.S. Department of Labor numbers show that the Washington area's 6.4 percent unemployment is the lowest of any large area in the nation. Washington area home prices are up 9 percent.[1]

The Washington economy is supercharged by the inflow of new federal government spending and the legal and lobbying business generated by the government proposing and issuing new federal laws and regulations. Even the quiet missions of Washington trade associations are growing as the government rushes to legislate and regulate. Americans outside Washington are paying ever more to Washington-based experts to explain massive 2,000-page bills as well as multitudes of proposed rules.

More than 10,000 lobbyists are formally registered to lobby the federal government. Interest groups, including unions, businesses, and the AARP, reported spending $3.5 billion in 2009 to

---

1 Murray, Sara. "City Unemployment: Vegas, Washington at Opposite Ends." *The Wall Street Journal.* July 28, 2010.

influence the federal government, and likely even more was spent in 2010.

American Bar Association statistics reveal that the number of "active, resident" lawyers in Washington, D.C., jumped from 46,689 in 2008 to 48,456 in 2009. This increase is the second highest in the nation, with only New York adding more lawyers. Washington, D.C. now has one lawyer for every twelve D.C. residents. This is more than ten times the rate of the next most-lawyered state, New York, which has one lawyer for every 127 citizens.

Why the large number and growth in lawyers and lobbyists? The Obama Administration and Congress have been legislating and regulating to a degree unparalleled in our lives. This fuels the Washington metropolitan area economy, making it the nation's wealthiest area by almost every definition, even as the rest of the national economy struggles. And the Washington boom will continue as the federal government hires thousands of new employees to implement the mandates of the health-care and financial reform bills as well as many little-noticed new bills.

Forbes.com reports that six of the ten wealthiest counties in the nation surround Washington, D.C. Washington, that most unique of American cities, is ever growing, ever expanding.[2] It does not know recessions because it does not produce anything consumers can reject. You must purchase what Washington is selling. You pay for your required purchases with taxes, which feed Washington more than any other city in the country.

Indeed, it is the best of times for our nation's capital.

For Detroit, it is the worst of times and has been for some time. Over the last fifty years, the city has lost more than half its population. Despite an influx of Washington stimulus cash, the 2010 Census shows that Detroit is still bleeding residents, losing over 1,700 people

---

2   Levy, Francesca. "America's 25 Richest Counties." *Forbes.com*. March 4, 2010.

in 2009, second only to Cleveland.[3] As they say, people vote with their feet, and the flight from Detroit mirrors a larger national trend, with states like Michigan, New York, and Illinois suffering net population losses over the past ten years. People go where there's opportunity, and there simply isn't any in Detroit.

What a difference a couple of decades make. In my lifetime, albeit when I was young, Detroit represented the epitome of the American Dream. It was a destination city for entrepreneurs, innovators, executives, blue-collar workers, and thousands of poor African Americans fleeing the bigotry of the Jim Crow South. Now, the children of those dream-seekers can't wait to leave.

As I leave the Detroit airport to see my family, the anecdotal evidence bears this out. The unprecedented number of "for sale" signs, abandoned buildings, and empty lots tell the story of Detroit's vast decline. ABC News reported that, in March 2010, more than 33,000 Detroit homes were believed to be vacant.[4]

Meanwhile, the economic numbers reveal a city struggling with high unemployment and a flaccid business environment. In the summer of 2010, Detroit's unemployment rate was over 20 percent, twice as high as the national average. And even before the current economic downturn, Detroit led major metropolitan areas in unemployment trauma. Between 2000 and the first quarter of 2010, Detroit lost over 270,000 jobs, making it the worst out of 363 job markets measured by the U.S. Conference of Mayors.

Of course, Detroit's decline is tied to the absolute and relative decline of the Big Three auto manufacturers, which remain the city's largest employers. Fifty years ago, these distinctly American companies were the Dells, Microsofts, and Apples of the American

3   Brown, Angela. "Flint Number 3 in U.S. for Population Loss." *ABC News 12, WJRT.* June 22, 2010.

4   Williams, Corey. "Detroit Fires Add to Burned, Vacant Landscape." *ABC.com.* September 9, 2010.

economy. Although the United States didn't invent the automobile, this country made it its own—indeed, never in the history of mankind had such an advanced technological achievement been available to so many. The American car in the middle of the twentieth century was what the personal computer would be at the end: one in every home.

And although the car is very much still with us, Detroit's day is, as I look out the window, all but over. It survives only by the largesse of that other city I call home: Washington. The relative opulence of Washington compared to the distress of Detroit epitomizes a challenged nation. With apologies to Dickens, this tale of two cities is the story of the expansion of the public sector and the decay of the private sector. It is the story of how the public sector, ever growing, feeds on the wealth generated by the private sector. It is the story of how a once great American industry now must beg, hat in hand, at the table of Washington.

And it's a tale I see all over the country, not just on my weekly trips back and forth between Detroit and Washington. Detroit, once the most innovative city in the country, is dying, and America's innovative spirit is dying with it. In its place are the lawyers and lobbyists of Washington, who spend their work days trying to get the largest share of the Washington handout of taxpayers' money.

It's the story of the decline of America.

THE FAILURE OF A GENERATION

My parents' generation worked hard to give my generation, the so-called Baby Boomers, a better world. They worked hard so we could be educated. They endured depressions and fought wars to give us a better future. They sacrificed so we would have a better life. They died knowing they gave it their all, did the right thing, and succeeded.

Sadly, my generation will not pass on with the comforting thought that we have done our children well. We are the first American generation that has failed to sacrifice for the next generation. Instead, we have stolen from them. We have lived for today. Every jobs bill, unemployment payments extension, corporate bailout, subsidy of state liabilities, and stimulus package; every increase in public pensions, Medicare, Social Security, and prescription drug and health-care coverage is a new debt we pile on our children. These benefits, which we bestow on ourselves, lift us briefly. But they massively burden our children and their children.

And with each heralded calamity, we focus on how to spend more money that we don't have rather than on the opportunity to make tough choices and solve long-term problems. Instead, the crisis is an opportunity for a politician to fund his favorite spending program or for Congress to build another layer of bureaucracy. We can summarize this attitude of ours with the words from President Obama's first White House Chief of Staff, Rahm Emanuel: "Never let a crisis go to waste."

Which is why our children will be the first generation of Americans to inherit a more difficult life. While they will be enriched by technology, they will be poorer by other, more important measures. They will inherit a nation with more debt, less wealth, and greater challenges. More, they may not be equipped to deal with the intense competitiveness of a global economy.

We are already seeing burdens we put on our children and grandchildren. Spending and pension obligations at the municipal level are forcing cities to cut somewhere, and so we see austerity measures like "Furlough Fridays" for students and teachers, reduced foreign language and music courses, and larger classrooms with fewer instructors. These cuts are a transfer of wealth from the young to the old. We are now cannibalizing our children's education to pay for our retirement. This is intergenerational theft. We are greedy geezers.

Our generation is but a link in the chain of generations. But now we are the weakest link. We have blithely assumed that our nation, which has been great, will continue to be great without our making it so. That is the curse of success: We assume prosperity is just something that happens, not something you work for. We had better start working, or history will record us as the generation that destroyed our children's future.

Right now, the future looks pretty bleak. As I survey the economic, political, and social elements of America at the moment, I don't see a society prepared to face a more competitive, more interconnected global future. The United States is drowning in debt, its political leaders are focused on false solutions, and we are failing to prepare our next generation to confront tomorrow's challenges.

In short, we are deliberately pushing our nation into a decline. But before we can talk about arresting that decline, we have to properly and honestly assess the severity of our problems. And those problems begin with our economy.

BEWARE THE GREEKS

For decades now, the United States, supported by a stable political system and a growing private sector, has been able to avoid economic realities. Policies and habits that would undo a lesser country are standard operating procedure in the United States, precisely because our underlying economic and political foundations have been sound. But the party is ending.

Although Greece's output is just over 2 percent of the European Union economy, its financial collapse in the first half of 2010 roiled continental markets and required an international bailout. Imagine what would happen to U.S. markets if California, which is 13 percent of the national economy, experienced a Greek-style implosion.

A study by a group at Stanford University pegs California's unfunded pension liabilities at $500 billion. But that only includes California's own state debt. When you factor in California's 13 percent stake in the U.S. economy, which is saddled with $13 trillion in debt, the state's total debt liability is over $2 trillion.

In many ways, California as a state has bigger problems than Greece as a country. The unemployment rate in California is higher than that of Greece. Much has been made of the ability of Greek government workers to retire at the age of fifty-three. In California, government workers can retire at fifty-five. As defeated gubernatorial candidate Meg Whitman noted during her campaign, the amount California spends on its pension programs has increased by 2,000 percent in the last decade to over $7 billion annually.[5] More, while California lost over one million private sector jobs since 2007, California's public employment has remained flat.[6]

In fact, if California were an independent nation, it probably would have suffered Greece's fate a long time ago. The only thing keeping California—and Michigan, and Illinois, and New York—afloat is the resiliency of the U.S. economy, which is the best long-term bet in the world.

Or at least it used to be.

According to White House estimates, our total federal government debt will be $20.3 trillion by 2020.[7] But this doesn't factor in the unfunded liabilities associated with Medicare and Social Security. Also, this burden assumes no further crises, wars, or bailouts of state and local governments over the next ten years—not exactly realistic assumptions. This 2020 debt amount—$20.3 trillion—is

---

5   Whitman, Meg. "California Pension Reform." *NationalReviewOnline.com*. April 23, 2010.

6   Schwarzenegger, Arnold. "Public Pensions and Our Fiscal Future." *Wall Street Journal*. August 27, 2010.

7   "CBO Report: Debt will rise to 90% of GDP." *Washington Times*. March 26, 2010.

if nothing changes at all. And the interest alone on $20.5 trillion, roughly $500 billion per year, would swallow about a third of today's entire federal budget. The Congressional Budget Office (CBO) says that if we keep on this path, we will raise the federal debt to 90 percent of the nation's economic output by 2020.

How will our huge annual string of deficits and growing total debt affect us?

Well, take your pick. There's the example of Japan, which suffered in the 1990s from what was known as the "lost decade." Following a real estate crunch in the early part of the decade, Japan responded with massive stimulus packages to boost economic growth. To offset the rising deficits these spending packages created, Japan had to raise taxes, which destroyed the fragile recovery and ensured that the crisis continued for several more years.

Or we could follow the scenario of present-day Greece. As our federal deficits continue to grow unchecked, the international community will eventually lose confidence in the U.S. government as a good investment. Our debt rating will go down, our interest expense will increase, the federal government will impose austerity, and government workers will revolt.

As quickly as Greece collapsed, the United States could find itself a second-rate economic power. The dollar's replacement as the world's reserve currency would be the least of our problems. Rebuilding America's credit would take precedence over any other domestic priority, which would require taxes at least twice as high as they are now. In short, the private sector would exist to rebuild the public sector—at least, much more than it already does. America's economic engine would sputter for decades.

Or more immediately, we will see states and local governments facing a condition equivalent to bankruptcy. These governments survived 2009 and 2010 thanks to receiving one-third of the $787 billion stimulus package, courtesy of the U.S. taxpayer, plus another late 2010 bailout from Congress in the form of Medicaid and unemployment insurance assistance. Predictably this has allowed the worst offenders—California, New York, and Illinois—to delay addressing their structural problems of bloated state payrolls and huge pension obligations and they still look to Uncle Sam. California's 2011 budget simply assumes an additional $5 billion gift from Congress. The Ponzi scheme can't continue, and it won't continue.

Whether we're talking about federal or state obligations, those debts must be paid—or, more realistically, the federal and state governments must at least put forth a good-faith effort to control our debts and begin to live within their means. We have seen what happens when those debts are called in: Beware the Greeks.

DEMOCRATS CAN'T ADD; REPUBLICANS CAN'T SUBTRACT

But are our political leaders honest (and mature) enough to address our economic and budgetary problems in a forthright and realistic way? Are they prepared to do what my parents' generation did and accept that *sacrifice* is required?

Given the last few years, there's no reason to think they will.

Across the ideological spectrum, our political leadership has become more political and less leader. With a different crisis dominating the headlines every week—from bankruptcies to bailouts, from bonuses to stimulus packages, from global warming to health care, from unemployment to madmen terrorists, from education to oil spills—our political leaders run about like chickens without heads. There is no coherent focus in Washington; there's just politics. Consider the last two years of major policy changes, which have come too swiftly to comprehend:

- ▶ **The 2008 TARP bill.** Total cost: $700 billion. Total debate time: TARP passes Congress in two weeks.
- ▶ **The 2009 stimulus package.** Total cost: $787 billion. Total debate time: The House voted ten hours after the bill was printed.
- ▶ **The 2010 "Obamacare."** Total cost: Unknown. Total debate time: House voted three days after bill was introduced.

To be fair, Congress did debate "Obamacare" at great length, several months in fact from end-to-end. But the problem was that the debate was never really about what was in the bill. Why? Because no one knew what was in the bill. As then–House Speaker Nancy Pelosi said—all too truthfully, as it would turn out—"We have to pass the bill so that you can find out what is in it."

Indeed, within two months of the vote, the CBO "reissued" its scoring by adding over $115 billion in costs.[8] No one (other than the White House on its Web site) even pretends any more that "Obamacare" will be "revenue neutral," which is how the Democratic leadership persuaded wavering members to sign on. To this day, we still can't say with any confidence how this bill will radically transform the American health-care system. Democrats think they know; Republicans think otherwise. This is what passes for serious and honest debate in Washington these days.

At the heart of our political impasses are the governing habits (I hesitate to call them philosophies) of the two parties. Democrats, we all know, are fond of being for the "little guy." They believe in a taxation and spending model that, in their view, achieves a more equitable distribution of wealth. As such, they spend like drunken sailors, with little regard for the consequences of giving everyone everything (except of course "the rich").

---

8   "Discretionary Spending in the Final Health Care Legislation." *Congressional Budget Office.* May 11, 2010.

Meanwhile, Republicans are great believers in the free market and limited government. But the largest explosion of government prior to the passage of "Obamacare" occurred under the Bush Administration and a Republican-controlled Congress. Although they passed tax cuts and tore down trade and regulatory barriers to business, they didn't have the political courage to enact serious spending cuts.

Our political problem is that Democrats can't add, and Republicans can't subtract. Democrats spend a lot and, when they can, raise taxes. Republicans won't raise taxes, but they won't cut spending. If you won't raise taxes and won't cut anything, then the cancerous deficit grows.

Think about it: The 2008 presidential contest was fought between a Republican who promised no new taxes and didn't advocate cutting any major government programs and a Democrat who promised the largest expansion of government since LBJ's Great Society and no new taxes for anyone making less than $250,000. We are looting from our children and grandchildren, and we had to choose between two candidates who were unwilling to even raise the tough issues.

Neither party has a real strategy focused on the long-term health of the nation. Rather, each has a philosophy and a set of programs designed for today. But what would you expect from a government full of Baby Boomers?

DO AS WE SAY, NOT AS WE DO

And what about that next generation, the one I'm so concerned my generation is, for want of a better phrase, stealing from?

On the one hand, this next generation is putting us all to shame. Since September 11, over 1.5 million Americans, a vast majority of them under twenty-five years old, have served in Iraq and

Afghanistan.[9] Many were in grade school when the Twin Towers fell, and yet they still took our nation's wars upon themselves. It is awe-inspiring, and it is a sign of the greatness of this country that we still produce so many brave young people willing to serve.

On the other hand, because the rest of the rising generation is taking its sweet time to start acting and working like adults, many in my generation think they're all a bunch of spoiled slackers. Indeed, 40 percent of twenty-somethings move back home, and nearly 30 percent fail to pay their bills on time. Twenty percent of the rising generation is carrying credit card debt exceeding $10,000.[10]

Meanwhile, in the 1970s, the median marrying age was twenty-one for women, twenty-three for men. Today, the median age is twenty-six for women, and twenty-eight for men. A new term has been coined in academic circles to describe this period of one's life: "emerging adult."

It conjures a particularly disturbing image:

Dad: "Hey, son. You're a twenty-five-year-old college graduate. Why are you sleeping on our couch?"
Son: "Get with the times, Dad. I'll get my own place, but right now I'm 'emerging.'"

It would be easy to put the blame on the son in this scenario, if the economic prospects for the rising generation weren't so bleak. Throughout 2010, the unemployment rate for workers under twenty-five was consistently double the national rate, usually in the 20 percent area. Moreover, this generation is graduating college

---

9   "Obama: The American combat mission in Iraq has ended." *CNN.com*. August 31, 2010.

10   Henig, Robin Marantz. "What Is It About 20-Somethings? 'Why are so many people in their 20s taking so long to grow up?'". *New York Times*. August 18, 2010.

with an average of $23,000 in student debt. Throughout the current economic downturn, about 37 percent of eighteen- to twenty-nine-year-olds have been underemployed, which is the highest share in three decades, according to a Pew Research Poll.

Whose fault is all this? It certainly isn't theirs. They weren't the ones creating bad policy. They weren't the ones defaulting on a home mortgage they never should have signed. They weren't the ones spending more than they had, in the false belief that the good times were here to stay. That's all our fault. And it gets worse:

- ► Thirty-one Organization for Economic Cooperation and Development (OECD) countries scored higher, on average, than the U.S. in mathematics literacy.
- ► U.S. students scored lower on science literacy than their peers in sixteen of the other twenty-nine OECD countries. [11]
- ► Only 31 percent of U.S. bachelor's degrees are awarded in science or engineering. (Japan's rate is more than double ours.)

We fail to educate our children to compete in a global world. Too few younger Americans have critical science and math training. Even fewer speak Arabic, Chinese, or Farsi—the languages of the future global economy. Our colleges prepare too few children for twenty-first-century jobs.

And then we leave them with a mountain of debt. How can we expect the next generation to have it better than we had it if we're teaching them all the wrong lessons? It's simple: We can't, and they won't.

---

11   United States. U.S. Department of Education. *Highlights From PISA 2006: Performance of U.S. 15-Year-Old Students in Science and Mathematics Literacy in an International Context.* December 2007.

THE AMERICAN DREAM, REVISITED

This is why I have taken the time to survey for the reader the state of America at the end of the first decade of the twenty-first century, because we are in danger of forfeiting that which has made us uniquely great: the American Dream. The United States is not great because our armies have conquered the world. We are not great because our boundaries extend farther than any other country's boundaries.

We are great because we offer anyone who comes here a simple deal: Work hard in our free society, and your children will have the opportunity for a better life than you had. That's the American Dream, at least as millions upon millions of immigrants have understood it. And that's what we are in danger of losing: Our children will not have it better than we did.

We have been shortsighted and reckless. We must acknowledge that, with our annual deficits and cumulative debt, America is in decline. From the Greeks and Romans to the French and English, history has followed the same pattern. Strong growth, optimism, and confidence transform into arrogance, entitlement, and complacency. The people, enamored of their standard of living, demand for free what their parents worked for. In turn, eager, prudent, and clever nations rise and replace the old ones.

If we want to preserve the American Dream, we need a framework for America's future. We need an action plan that builds on our strengths and minimizes our weaknesses. It must be executed over the long term—I'm talking decades. And yes, it requires sacrifice for a better future.

Fortunately, the way forward isn't a total secret. It's the same path Americans from every age have followed. We are a nation of pioneers and innovators. We aim higher and go further than any other people on the globe. We look at barriers and see opportunity; we look at our lives and want to make them better.

What separates America from any other nation on the planet? Just this: We give our citizens the freedom to succeed, or at least we used to, and we reward those who see further or more creatively than anyone else. It's what I call innovation, and it's the key to our current troubles. It's what built once-great cities like Detroit, and its decline is what has ruined them. Innovation is the engine of human progress, and for the last one hundred years, America has led that progress. It's time to lead once again.

Our parents did their job. Let us do ours. This is our time.

2

Why Innovation?

"Video won't be able to hold on to any market it captures after the first six months. People will soon get tired of staring at a plywood box every night."

—DARRYL F. ZANUCK, 20th Century Fox,
commenting on television in 1946

THE VCR WARS

Of all the failed predictions —uttered throughout history, Zanuck's dismissal of the television in its earliest years isn't the most laughable, but it's pretty darn close. We could look at the numbers and the statistics to embarrass Zanuck even further, but why bother? You know the score: that "plywood box" changed history.

Instead, let me tell the story of a less well known dismissal of a transformational innovation, in which I played a role, albeit minor. My career representing technology innovators effectively began in the late 1970s when a group of Hollywood movie studios sued Sony for making and selling a device called the video cassette recorder (VCR).

I was a hungry Georgetown law student struggling to make ends meet when Ed Day, a senior partner at the firm Squire, Sanders and Dempsey, took me under his wing. Day was an innovator himself, having introduced the zip code while postmaster general under President Kennedy, back when the postmaster general was a cabinet position.

Day called me into his big corner office overlooking Pennsylvania Avenue in D.C., and told me about the lawsuit brought by Hollywood against Sony and various retailers who were making and selling the VCR. He asked me to follow the lawsuit and any related activity.

As detailed in the book *Fast Forward* by Jim Lardner, the predecessor to the VCR was a bulky tape machine invented by Ampex, a California company. Primarily used by broadcasters, the Ampex device was modestly successful but had not been sold in a smaller, consumer product version.

After Sony first started selling a consumer version—the Betamax—in 1976, Hollywood sued and sought an injunction on VCR sales. The studios claimed that copyright laws gave them the exclusive right to make copies of their product and that the VCR, by allowing consumers to record over-the-air broadcast television for free, violated their copyright and made Sony a "contributory infringer" through its innovation.

The VCR allowed "time shifting," and for the first time consumers had control of what they could watch and when they could watch it. This freedom to control content was what so concerned Hollywood executives. Their successful history had relied on total control of distribution and showing of their movies and TV programs. If consumers could record the annual TV broadcast of *The Wizard of Oz* and watch it whenever they wanted, then why would advertisers pay broadcasters the following year? Hollywood's fear was real and understandable.

But it was still wrong.

In 1979, a federal court in California rejected Hollywood's claims. We breathed a sigh of relief. But then Hollywood appealed to the

Ninth Circuit Court of Appeals, which overturned the lower court's ruling and held that the VCR was an illegal product. The fight then went to the Supreme Court.

Those of us defending the VCR immediately went into action and created the Home Recording Rights Coalition (HRRC). This group of manufacturers (including 3M, GE, and RCA), retailers (Sears and others), and consumer groups began meeting weekly to figure out how to reverse this legal action, which we all knew was fatal to a compelling new innovation.

The HRRC retained former Federal Communications Commission chairman Charlie Ferris and former senator Marlow Cook. Several companies hired their own lawyers. One group of companies hired a troika of then relatively unknown lawyers who since have each significantly changed America: Ron Brown, then a partner at Patton Boggs, later headed the Democratic Party and tragically died in a 1996 plane crash while serving as secretary of commerce; David Rubenstein, then in private practice but formerly the clever but self-effacing aide to President Carter, went on to create the Carlyle Group, the world's largest private equity firm; and Former Justice Department lawyer Bob Schwartz, a brilliant legal writer and aspiring saxophonist, went on to found an independent record label and has been protecting innovation for three decades.

In 1981, this group of lawyers and strategists began meeting at least once a week to plot our legislative and legal strategy. The meetings were amazing debates on philosophy and strategy. Who could be our allies? Which legislators might be sympathetic? Who would talk to them? What approach would work depending on their party, known views, and constituents? With Democrats, the default was protecting consumers. With Republicans, it was protecting the free market, fledgling businesses, and innovation. We created charts of the 535 legislators and assigned responsibility for contacting them. We sought the aid of consumer groups, think tanks, retailers, and even a sympathetic priest willing to put his name on letters. I became part of this inner circle almost immediately. Considering my notable lack of qualifications, other than my ignorant youthful confidence, in retrospect, it is amazing they accepted me.

Immediately following the Ninth Circuit's decision, Congress sprang to action. Senator Dennis DeConcini, an Arizona Democrat, introduced a simple bill reversing the decision. But Senator Charles Mathias, a Maryland Republican, responded with a seventeen-page bill allowing VCRs to be sold if the manufacturers paid a royalty tax to the content providers. At the bottom of the Mathias bill was a paragraph stating that the "first sale doctrine" for video products would be repealed. That paragraph turned out to be a game changer.

The "first sale" doctrine means that the copyright owner can only control the "first sale" of a copyrighted work—from a bookstore to a consumer, for example. After that, the consumer can do what he chooses with that specific book—give it away, sell it, or trade it for another book.

After a little research, I discovered that this seemingly innocuous paragraph actually signified a radical change in the American concept of personal property. Unlike all other copyright holders, movie studios would now be permitted to control their product after the first sale. Simply, this provision, if made into law, would have barred video rentals.

Video stores were just appearing, and in several cities groups of owners had formed regional associations to protect their interests. I decided to travel the country to meet with the store owners and, well, stir them up a bit over Hollywood's attempt to put them out of business. The result was the creation of the Video Software Dealers Association, which gave us the critical ability to create a real grassroots movement that could serve as a counterweight to Hollywood in the lobbying halls of Congress.

Amazingly, while developing and executing this strategy, I faced off against one respected lawyer who represented a major VCR manufacturer. She disagreed with my assessment that we had a very clear interest in video rentals and that it was an integral part of the case. I countered that we needed the grassroots support because the manufacturers and retailers of VCRs comprised a fledgling, exciting new retail industry, and that killing it with the oppressive hand of government went against everything we were fighting for. When she failed to convince me, she sought out my association client and asked that I be removed from representing the association. The feisty Jack Wayman, a WWII vet and Purple Heart recipient who headed the HRRC through his position at what was then the predecessor to the Consumer Electronics Association, not only stood by me, but he also asked me to join the association full time as its first in-house lawyer lobbyist.

This was a personal turning point. My mentor Ed Day cautioned me that associations were "where you go to retire," implying a drop in status and possibly damaging my career in its infancy. But, in truth, the decision was easy. I had already attended my first Consumer Electronics Show and never felt such energy or seen so much innovation. I hungered to be part of the fledgling consumer electronics industry.

Moreover, I was captivated by the inner workings of innovation. What do I mean? Just this: Even when you have the most exciting new innovation on the market, that's no guarantee it—or you—will be successful. Innovation by its very definition undermines the status quo. It can destroy jobs, markets, and entire industries. For every consumer who drooled at the VCR concept, there was a well-connected power broker determined to block it.

We like to think that the invisible hand of the free market works without our conscious intervention, but this is a fallacy. In truth, all sorts of artificial obstacles stand in the way of technological progress—foremost among them the coercive hand of government. We might regret this, but we also should remember that one's right to build the next great mousetrap is just as important as someone else's right to vocally oppose it and lobby the government on his behalf.

In any event, in the middle of the VCR battle, I determined that I wanted to be on the side of innovation, of progress. I wanted to represent the technological pioneers of this great country as they went about their business of seeing further than anyone else—which is, I believe, the business of America.

Upon joining the association full time, I shifted from strategizing lawyer to decision maker, peacekeeper, and the outside face for the cause of innovation in technology. Although Wayman chaired the HRRC, I was made vice chairman, and given his frequent travels, I ended up running the HRRC weekly meetings and being chief spokesmen for the cause.

Those were heady days. I was leading an army of some of the top lawyers and lobbyists in Washington. More, we were up against the most powerful lobby in town, the Motion Picture Association of America (MPAA), headed by the legendary Jack Valenti. With his background as a top aide to President Johnson and his reputation for oration and influence, Valenti and the movie studios attacked us and the VCR as the death of American movies.

But in the end, Valenti and Hollywood lost. In a hair-raising 5–4 decision, the Supreme Court ruled in *Sony v. Universal Studios* (1984) that VCRs did not violate the Copyright Act of 1976. Importantly, the Court found that a recording did not automatically infringe a copyright on a broadcast movie even if it was used to make a full copy of the movie. The Court's ruling was more than my first legal victory for innovation; it represented a major leap forward in the quickly expanding industry of consumer electronics. Although the battle shifted then from the Court to Congress, in the end we won for three reasons:

First, we were right. Although innovation can be a painful process, protecting the status quo industries would lead to even greater harm. Imagine if the horse-and-buggy industry had managed to block the automobile industry. Imagine if the locomotive industry had been able to block Orville and Wilbur Wright. Had one justice voted the other way, it would have signaled the death knell for an exciting new technology—one that presented challenges, yes, but one that also grew into one of the largest industries in the country.

Second, we were smart and strategic. We knew we couldn't match the huge political fundraising of Hollywood or the plush MPAA screening room across from the White House used to show first-run movies and to lobby politicians. We weren't sexy, so we had to be smart. We had a talented team, and we invested a huge amount of time developing a strategy and the intellectual framework for our cause. While our Hollywood opponents appeared overly confident, insular, with a top-down approach and a simple message—protect this great American industry from the devil's technology—we were the entrepreneurial underdog, fighting for survival.

Third, we were underestimated. Our opponent was an established American industry, which in Washington always has the advantage. This forced us to create an intensely collaborative work environment, where all opinions could be aired. And what a group we had!

In addition to those named earlier, the frighteningly funny Wayne Berman, now chairman of Ogilvy Government Relations, lightened up our meetings, along with thoughtful former FCC lawyers Jeff Cunard and Bob Bruce and colorful former Food and Drug Administration counsel Nancy Buc. Also adding to our intellectual and strategic heft were the highly respected Washington lawyers Bruce Turnbull, Gary Slaiman, Jonathan Potter, and Jeff Turner, and our association strategist Michael Petricone. Economist Nina Cornell, executive director Ruth Rodgers, PR maven

Allan Schlosser, and grassroots entrepreneur Jack Bonner rounded out the team.

Our weekly meetings averaged over twenty people, and although I was privileged to lead them, I also couldn't resist calculating that each hour of each meeting costs clients thousands of dollars in lawyers' time. But the expense of the team was justified because so much was at stake—more than I even reckoned at the time. I thought we were just fighting for the survival of the VCR; it turns out that if we had lost, there would be no iPod, camcorder, DVR, PVR, and arguably only a limited Internet. The VCR was a gateway technology, and making sure that the doorway remained opened has led to more economic expansion than anything we could have predicted then.

It's funny the way some moments in your life have the ability to change you, while others, seemingly more consequential, do not. Looking back thirty years later, I now realize that my experience in the VCR wars has shaped so much of the way I look at the world today, if only because the consequences of failure would have been so profound. But that's the way of innovation: if we had lost we wouldn't have known what we missed. We know now, and it's the reason I'm writing this book.

AN ARMY OF STEAMROLLERS

But what do I mean by innovation? Clearly, as president and CEO of the Consumer Electronics Association, my experience with innovation has focused on the next great gadget—the VCR, computers, the iPod, HDTV, BluRay, smartphones, etc. A lot of people look at these things and dismiss them as high-tech toys—most ardently when the next "must-have" gadget first enters the market. They're exciting but "not something I'll waste money on."

What many of those same folks forget is that yesterday's toys are often today's tools; the novelty becomes necessary. When the first personal computers were introduced in the early 1970s, they were the things of hobbyists and techno-geeks (if they'll excuse the term). Cool, interesting, but *what do you do with it?* Today, three out of four Americans own one. Twenty-five years ago, people dismissed cell phones. Clunky, poor reception, and *why do I need one?* Today, over 90 percent of U.S. households own one.

So to the question: What is innovation? Innovation is progress. Innovation is growth. Innovation is the engine of the free market. Above all, innovation is necessary. Ninety percent of U.S. households own a cell phone, not because the owners enjoy talking on a cell phone, but because they *need* it.

But there's an ugly side to innovation, as well. Innovation destroys—in many cases, viciously. When was the last time you wrote on a typewriter or used a travel agent? Or used a phone booth?

But those phone booths and typewriters didn't appear out of thin air. Someone had to make them, and he or she was employed by a company, which was owned by a board, which had an obligation to stock holders, who used their profits to provide for their families. All of it is gone today, destroyed because someone else invented a phone that at first fit in your briefcase. Now it fits in your pocket.

But that's the way of innovation. It's what the economist Joseph Schumpeter called "creative destruction." Perhaps more so than in any other nation, it's been an integral force in America since our very founding. When I think about the story of America, I can't help but remember James Earl Jones' memorable speech in the movie *Field of Dreams*: "America has rolled by like an army of steamrollers. It's been erased like a blackboard, rebuilt, and erased again."

The point Jones was making was about the permanence of baseball and the importance of a true American heritage. But I've always liked the other point Jones was making, if not deliberately: America is not an idle nation, and Americans aren't idle people. We are restive. We are impatient. We want more, and we want it better. Our identity isn't locked in an old cathedral built centuries ago. It isn't preserved in scrolls dug from the ground or inscribed on ancient temples.

Our identity is preserved in the people who came to this continent to build a better life, and what they left us was a better country. Their ideas and their talents transformed our nation and pushed us from a ragtag bunch of farmer revolutionaries to the largest economy on earth. Each wave that reached these shores, each "army of steamrollers," remade America with its creative energy and desire to live the American Dream.

As one army of steamrollers rolls by, erasing, destroying, it is also creating, rebuilding, progressing. And then the next army comes and starts the process all again. And it's been going on for over two hundred years. Think of the breakthroughs: electricity, the telephone, the television, and the Internet. Each one by itself radically transformed life as people of that time knew it. These innovations changed our world.

But what do these innovations share, besides causing radical change?

First, they were developed by American ingenuity. Americans are the world's innovators. Our supremacy as innovators is at risk, and we must recognize why we are innovators and focus on preserving the conditions that foster innovation. This book is about what it takes to keep America the world's leader in innovation.

Second, innovation challenges the status quo. Old businesses and jobs don't like being threatened. They fight back. If they are smart, they also innovate. The cable industry innovated when satellite came along. They succeeded and survived because they expanded cable to embrace another innovation—the Internet—and quickly became the broadband provider to most of America. By adopting a new innovation, cable ensured its survival in the satellite age—at least until *wireless* broadband becomes a viable alternative. And so the steamrollers roll on.

Now compare cable's response to the broadcasting industry. Rather than adapting, the broadcasters often meet new competitive threats by lobbying government for more protection. For example, broadcasters have been urging Congress to pass a law mandating that all cell phones come with radio tuners. This absurdity would penalize the innovation of the cell phone with the antiquity of the FM radio and antennae.

Third, innovation creates jobs, even as it destroys others. Think of the news media, particularly the newspaper industry. The advent of the Internet has radically upended the newspaper business model. From the loss of subscriptions to classifieds, newspapers simply haven't figured out how to make a buck from selling news anymore. Entire newspapers have had to shut down or end their "dead tree" service.

Most major newspapers have experimented with different pricing models—only to see profits continue to fall. Some, like *The Wall Street Journal*, have prospered through sheer journalistic excellence. Sadly, the newspaper industry, as we knew it, is gone. But don't confuse my sadness for any hesitation that innovation and its twin, change, are healthy for the overall economy. Few would contend that the destruction of the newspaper industry cancels out the wealth-creating and job-producing effects of the Internet. It's not even close. The industry is merely a casualty of innovation, at least for now. Who knows what some pioneering, innovative mind will come up with to save newspapers and reverse their decade-long decline? Believe me, many are trying, and someone will succeed.

These past thirty years, I have been at the center of some of the most fundamental changes in the technologies that consumers use and enjoy. I have participated in various ways in the development and launch of dozens of new technologies and products. Some, like the VCR, are museum relics. Others never even made it that far. But through it all, I have fought those seeking to maintain the status quo and protect their sliver of the market. On the other hand, I have also seen numerous examples of industries embracing change and adapting on their own.

It has been a joy and privilege to be at the pinnacle of an industry that has dramatically increased the world's pace of innovation. American innovators have opened billions of people to a richness of experience and knowledge that wasn't imaginable to the world's wealthiest a generation ago. Along the way, we created millions of jobs.

Innovation is our most important and uniquely American asset. Innovation *is* America. We didn't invent innovation—but it is our brand. It is what we do best.

WILL THE NEXT BILL GATES BE INDIAN OR CHINESE?

But are we protecting our brand? In the next decade, will the United States remain an economic leader, or will it be forced to take a backseat to rising global powers from other corners of the world? It is the general thesis of this book that we are in serious danger of losing the very thing Americans do better than anyone else—and have for two hundred years.

At least, that's what I think.

In 2010, the Consumer Electronics Association commissioned a poll from Zogby International of almost 4,000 American adults. Our chief concern was discovering just what Americans think about innovation. Is it on their minds? Do they care? Are they worried?

What we found confirms that most Americans believe we are at a crossroads when it comes to innovation. While we have a strong innovation economy today, Americans are uncertain if we will be able to maintain our competitive edge—especially in the face of untested policy decisions and the rising national debt. Consider some key findings:

Innovation is the key to future U.S. economic success. Ninety-six percent of Americans said that innovation was important to the U.S. being a world economic leader in the future. Young Americans, more than any other age group, felt the most strongly about the role innovation should play, with 87 percent of eighteen- to twenty-four-year-olds saying that it was "very important."

Innovation provides the key to U.S. competitiveness. A plurality, 44 percent, of Americans said that "remaining the most innovative country in the world" is the most important thing the United States can do to ensure its future success as a world leader. Twenty-two percent said it would be "remaining the largest economy in the world," while 15 percent said military power was most important.

Innovation will impact future careers. Sixty-eight percent of Americans believe that innovation is important to the future success of their place of employment, with 50 percent saying that innovation was important for their job remaining in the United States.

Young Americans look to the tech sector for future jobs. When asked which sector of the economy has the most potential for future job creation, nearly 50 percent of those aged eighteen to twenty-four said technology would lead the way over other sectors.

The next Bill Gates is most likely to come from India or China.
When asked where the "next Bill Gates will come from," 40
percent of Americans predicted either India or China.

So we know where most Americans stand on innovation. But for
the United States to lead the global economy, we need to pursue
national policies that encourage innovation, creativity, and new
ideas. For the United States to rise out of its current economic dol-
drums, we need to invest in technological innovation and create
an environment where entrepreneurs can challenge, improve, and
strengthen our society.

This book presents a plan to do just that. Spurring economic
growth and maintaining a competitive edge require more than
just tax cuts or onetime incentives. It is also not just about jobs. It
must become our goal as a nation to ensure that we have created
the necessary conditions to maintain our innovative dominance in
the world, which is the only realistic chance we have of keeping the
United States the strongest economic power in the world.

In short, we need to ensure that not just the next Bill Gates but
the fifty who come after him or her will innovate in America. English doesn't have to be their first language, but let's hope the United
States of America is on their passports.

This chapter began with my experience in the VCR wars and
how that experience has shaped my views on the importance
of innovation to our continued economic success. But the VCR
wars—and subsequent battles I've fought since then—have also
helped me see the process of innovation; namely, how a product
goes from being an idea to being in your home. It's a long process,
to be sure, full of obstacles and pitfalls and headaches and late,
late nights.

I don't pretend to know the secrets of innovation itself. You'll
have to ask a Steve Jobs about that. But I do know what it takes to

ensure that what a young innovator imagines becomes a reality—and how that reality creates wealth and jobs for millions of others.

What must we do to maintain and expand our innovation environment? What should we do as individuals, parents, schools, and legislators to maintain America's top position in the world? The rest of this book will provide answers.

If we want to guarantee our children the chance to live the American Dream, then we have to protect what is best about our nation: We have to save American innovation. Enough with the generalities, on to the specifics.

3

Innovation:
The Fuel of Economic Growth

"[I]f it should ever turn out that the basic logics of a machine designed
for the numerical solution of differential equations coincide with the
logics of a machine intended to make bills for a department store, I
would regard this as the most amazing coincidence that I have ever
encountered."

—COMPUTER PIONEER HOWARD AIKEN,
in congressional testimony in 1956

As RECOUNTED BY Nathan Rosenburg, a professor of economics at
Stanford University, in a 2004 paper for the OECD, this is precisely
what happened.[12] Those "machines designed for the numerical
solution of differential equations" (i.e., computers) coincided quite
nicely with what a teller machine did at a department store—not to
mention innumerable other machines.

But it wasn't a coincidence. Rosenburg's point is not to ridicule
Aiken, who was in fact a pioneer in computers, but to show that
sometimes even innovators themselves don't appreciate the real-
world (i.e., economic) value of the very thing they innovated.

---

12   Rosenburg, Nathan. "Innovation and Economic Growth." Stanford University. 2004.

Again, this isn't the fault of the innovators, whose minds aren't necessarily on getting rich. As Rosenburg writes, "The impact of a technological innovation will generally depend not only on its inventors, but also on the creativity of the eventual users of the new technology."

Sometimes the process is instantaneous, as with the Internet, whose economic appreciation occurred lightening-quick, relatively speaking. It took years for innovators and scientists to find an application for the laser.

Even economists have only in the last fifty or so years appreciated the full importance innovation has on the economic growth of a nation. Rosenburg traces this understanding back to the 1950s, when his colleague Professor Moses Abramovitz decided to measure the growth of output in the U.S. economy between 1870 and 1950.

> He then made what were thought to be reasonable assumptions about how much a growth in a unit of labour and how much a growth in a unit of capital should add to the output of the economy. It turned out that the measured growth of inputs (i.e., in capital and labor) between 1870 and 1950 could only account for about 15 % of the actual growth in the output of the economy. In a statistical sense, then, there was an unexplained residual of no less than 85%.[13]

In other words, what Abramovitz's models couldn't account for was the increase in output given the same number of inputs. Ignorance of the importance of innovation was also partly due to the generally inadequate data economists had to work with prior to the modern age. But Abramovitz's "residual" had intrigued other economists.

In 1957, American economist Robert Solow defined a break-

---

13   Ibid.

through analytical model of the U.S. economy that attributed over 80 percent of the growth in economic output per worker to "technical progress." Nevertheless, it took thirty more years before Solow was awarded the Nobel Prize in economics for his work.

Writes Rosenburg: "It was precisely the size of this residual that persuaded most economists that technological innovation must have been a major force in the growth of output in highly industrialised economies."

This is the primary reason why the U.S. must remain the most innovative nation on earth: because innovation is the fuel that powers economic growth. Most important, only innovation produces the type of growth that increases our national standard of living, officially known as growth in real gross domestic product (GDP) per capita. Unfortunately, this fundamental economic truth is not well understood by many of our citizens, including our politicians.

In large part, this is due to widespread ignorance of basic economics that has persisted since our nation's founding in 1776. Indeed, in that year, Adam Smith noted that "many improvements [in nations' wealth] have been made by the ingenuity of the makers of machines." Smith made this observation in his pioneering 1776 treatise known familiarly by its short title, *The Wealth of Nations*, one of the foundation texts of modern economics and well known to many of our founding fathers.

However, even though economic thinkers had no clear concept of innovation until recently, fortunately our innovators didn't notice. Eli Whitney's invention of the cotton gin in Georgia in 1793 fueled early creation of a massive national cotton and apparel industry. The building of a transcontinental railroad, completed in 1869, connected our vast continent and fostered growth in commerce among the states. Thomas Edison's invention of the incandescent light bulb and his efforts to build the electrical industry created the essential electric platform for industry development to the present day. The introduction of television in the early 1950s revolutionized entertainment, family life, and cultural habits, first here and then in most of the civilized world. In 1959, the first integrated circuit patents were filed in the United States, setting off a technology explosion that continues to this day.

So Americans were innovating from the very earliest days of our republic. But before examining the reasons the U.S. populace has been so creative, we should better understand what "innovation" actually means, in a strict economic sense (as opposed to the more general definition I used in the previous chapter).

WHAT IS INNOVATION?

One business dictionary defines it as the "process by which an idea or invention is translated into a good or service for which people will pay. To be called an innovation, an idea must be replicable at an *economic* cost and must satisfy a specific need." Thus, essential to the concept of innovation is that it must create incremental economic value. As the joke goes, a so-called innovation that does not create incremental value is generally called a failure.

The popular understanding of innovation focuses on new technologies such as those offered by major corporations like Intel, Microsoft, Apple, and Google, but innovation is much, much broader than that. Consider for example such relatively new firms as Starbucks, eBay, Staples, and PetSmart. In each case, the innovation was in the company business model and in how the company operated to create and serve its customers.

One useful way to think about the broad range of possible innovations is in terms of what is called the *business value chain*, the sequence of activities that a firm undertakes to create and serve customers. In this construct, innovation is possible in the entire range of business functions, including research, design, engineering, sourcing, production, distribution, marketing, sales, service, and so forth.

Yet despite this vast potential breeding ground for innovation, innovation remains relatively rare, especially those disruptive innovations that create new companies and even entire new industries. Innovation is particularly difficult for large companies and well-established companies, in part because they pay so much attention to defending what they have already achieved. Their innovation challenges have birthed a fairly large population of consultants, authors, and researchers eager to help these firms break out of their encrusted business habits. (Those consulting firms, in turn, each have their own well-established ways of doing things, but they need to be constantly innovating their practices as well.) Despite the difficulties of innovating, the U.S. has long led the world in innovation. For example, in technology hardware, we have Apple, Cisco, Dell, Intel, HP, Motorola, National Semiconductor, Nvidia, Qualcomm, and Texas Instruments. In software and services we have Accenture, IBM, Microsoft, and Oracle. Not only was the Internet invented here, but we also have the world's leading Internet-based companies, such as Amazon, Craigslist, Google, eBay, eTrade, Facebook, Flicker, Pandora, Twitter, and Yahoo.

We are also strong innovators in health care and related sciences. Our pharmaceutical, biotechnology, nanotechnology, aerospace, and chemical industries lead the world. Although we can complain about the costs, the fact is that the wealthiest people in the world journey to the United States to receive the best and most advanced medical treatments possible.

Moreover, the impressive U.S. innovation track record in industrial technology also extends to the creative arts. Hollywood dominates the world's big and small screens. Our independent studios make movies and TV programs. Our music industry and book and magazine writers and publishers are among the best and most prolific in the world.

Why does the U.S. lead the world in innovation, especially by such a wide margin? This issue has been much studied and debated, and I am persuaded that the answer lies in what has been called *American exceptionalism.* In my opinion, it is the fortunate result of our nation's rich and unique stew of individual liberty, constitutional democracy, limited government, free enterprise, social mobility, ethnic diversity, immigrant assimilation, intellectual freedom, property rights, and the rule of law. I can't deconstruct how each factor makes its individual contribution, but I believe each is vitally important.

I should also add that, in comparison to most of the industrialized world, Americans work harder. Despite the image of the pampered or spoiled American, the fact is that Americans on average work 1,776 hours per year. This is 467 more hours a year than Germany, 307 more hours than France, and 43 more hours than Japan. As Edison once said, success is 10 percent inspiration and 90 percent perspiration. We may also work smarter and be relatively more creative, but I don't know for certain.

Years ago, the Cato Institute examined certain specific factors that foster innovation. Researchers Thomas Jorde and David Teece wrote this:

Although the evidence is sketchy, factors that are important include: the availability of a labor force with the requisite technical skills; economic structures that permit considerable autonomy and entrepreneurship; economic systems that permit and encourage a variety of approaches to technological and market opportunities; access to "venture" capital, either from a firm's existing cash flow or from an external venture capital community; good connections between the scientific community, especially the universities, and the technological community, and between users and developers of technology; strong protection of intellectual property; the availability of strategies and structures to enable innovating firms to capture a return from their investment; and, in fragmented industries, the ability to quickly build or access cospecialized assets inside or outside the industry. [14]

Now that's a list, and I have no quarrel with most of it. But it seems to consist of factors that are and have been prevalent in other industrialized countries, so it doesn't necessarily explain the supremacy of *American* innovation. I think my list better accounts for America's innovation exceptionalism.

No other country has reached the U.S. level of creativity and innovation, and one result is that U.S. culture, language, and, to some extent, values have infiltrated other nations, multiplying the impact of our innovations themselves. This gives us global influence disproportionate to the size of our population and our economy, amplifying my concerns that innovation is too important to continue being less than an urgent national policy priority.

Thanks to many very smart people, we have a better, but not complete, understanding of how to foster innovation. But we also have a better understanding of how fragile our innovation leadership can be. And we see increasing threats to this leadership, and so to our economic health as well.

In February 2010, China announced it had issued a record number of patents in 2009: more than 580,000, a 41 percent increase from a year earlier.[15] Meanwhile, a September 2010 report from the United Nations' World Intellectual Property Organization announced that patent filing in the U.S. fell by 11.7 percent between 2008 and 2009.[16] Indeed, the drop in the United States—as in most

---

14   Jorde, Thomas M. and Teece, David J. "Innovation, Dynamic, Competition, and Antitrust Policy," Cato Institute, 1990.

15   Chao, Loretta. "China Issued Record Number of Patents in 2009." *The Wall Street Journal.* February 4, 2010.

16   Hindman, Nathaniel Cahners. "Innovation Shifted to China During the Downturn: U.N. Reports." *Huffington Post.* September 16, 2010.

developed nations—can be attributed to the global economic downturn, and will likely rise when the economy recovers.

But that's what makes China's growth so much more maddening.

To sustain and even enhance U.S. innovation, there are several essential and fundamental actions that I believe need to be taken, and these are addressed in the following chapters. These actions involve every important institution in our country, including education; federal, state and local legislators, and governments; industries large, small, and not yet created; law and the courts; labor; cultural centers; banks and private equity firms; and so on. Spurring action will require that each institution recognize the challenges, establish remedial goals, and fashion appropriate strategies. Qualified and energetic leadership is needed from the United States president on down.

We currently face a severe economic crisis, but like the Chinese, I believe every crisis contains the seeds of future success. "Innovate or die" was the concept I counseled companies about in the recent Great Recession. Some died, but many more innovated. A market cycle is tough, but it does weed out the weaker competitors and can certainly foster innovation.

The time for action is long past due.

4

Entrepreneurial Innovation: The Jobs Engine

"This summer, the America Recovery and Reinvestment Act (the 'Recovery Act') will shift its emphasis from short-term rescue efforts to long-term recovery and reinvestment projects. These projects will rebuild the infrastructure of today and break ground on the infrastructure of tomorrow, driving sustainable job creation, economic growth, innovation, and global competiveness."[17]

—SUMMER OF RECOVERY: Project Activity Increases in Summer 2010, Office of the Vice President, June 17, 2010

JOB CREATION

From the Department of Labor, the Bureau of Labor Statistics reported that the unemployment rate in the "Summer of Recovery" was:

- June: 9.5 percent
- July: 9.5 percent
- August: 9.6 percent[18]

---

17   United States. Office of the Vice President. *Summer of Recovery: Project Activity Increases in Summer 2010.* June 17, 2010.

18   U.S. Department of Labor, Bureau of Labor Statistics.

In September 2010, most Americans knew that the Obama Administration's "stimulus package" of nearly $1 trillion had failed in its principle task of restoring real economic growth and returning Americans to work. The administration's "Summer of Recovery" had become a "Summer of Embarrassment."

By the end of the summer, more and more stories like this one from the *Los Angeles Times* began cropping up:

Two L.A. agencies get $111 million in stimulus funds but have created only 55 jobs

September 17, 2010

Two Los Angeles departments have received $111 million in federal stimulus funds yet have created only 55 jobs so far, according to a pair of reports issued Thursday by City Controller Wendy Greuel.

The reports conclude that the agencies, Public Works and Transportation, moved too slowly in spending the federal money, in part because of the time it takes to secure approval of government contracts. The two agencies plan to create or retain a combined 264 jobs once all the money is spent, according to the reports.

With unemployment above 12%, city officials should move more urgently to cut red tape and spend the money, Greuel said. "The process needs to be changed to make sure we get these projects out as quickly as possible," she said . . .

So far, the public works agency has shielded 37 public employee jobs from elimination as a result of the city's ongoing budget crisis and created eight public or private jobs, the report said. Part of the problem, Greuel found, was that it took eight months to put together certain bid packages, review the bids and award the contracts. The second report looked at the Department of Transportation, which received seven grants worth nearly $41 million to purchase buses, install traffic signals and upgrade railroad crossings. Although those projects were designed to support 26 jobs, nine have been created or retained so far, Greuel's report said.[19]

Now imagine what a young start-up with a fresh new idea could have done with $111 million. I'm not advocating handouts to start-ups, but I am pointing out the absurdity behind the belief that government can spend its way to real job creation. The Office of the Vice President's report might have had the best of intentions, but those intentions always—always—run into the local Public Works and Transportation Offices, which haven't the foggiest idea how to create a job. That's why it spent over $2 million for each job it "created."

The U.S. economy is in crisis, with official "unemployment" stuck near 10 percent, and actual under-employment well into double digits, and both measures are dismally much higher for youths and minorities. Much of the public is frustrated that the federal government seems unable to stimulate real growth in our economy and jobs. Yet this presumes a fallacy—that it is the government's job to create jobs. Recently, the federal government's massive and quick action has caused so much business uncertainty and debt, it has actually reduced jobs.

To create the conditions for private entities to create jobs, the federal government should first do no harm. More, it can stimulate jobs by focusing on which environment is ready for innovation. The evidence of the unique economic power of innovation has been accumulating for most of our history and has become irrefutable as the high-technology revolution gained traction over the past several decades.

The news these days is filled with stories about how small business (defined by the federal government as firms having fewer than

---

19   Zahniser, David. "Two L.A. agencies get $111 million in stimulus funds but have created only 55 jobs." *Los Angeles Times*. September 17, 2010.

five hundred employees) is more responsible for driving job creation compared to larger businesses, and this is indisputably true. According to the U.S. Small Business Administration (SBA), small businesses account for a full 50 percent of total U.S. employment. Moreover, small businesses account for more than two-thirds of net new job creation.

I know firsthand the importance of small business in employment and job creation: 80 percent of the members of the Consumer Electronics Association are small businesses, and the International CES is similarly dominated by small businesses. But yet, company size is not the full story of job creation.

A 2010 study by the prestigious National Bureau of Economic Research concluded that only certain types of small business are the primary job creators:

> There's been a long, sometimes heated, debate on the role of firm size in employment growth . . . The widespread and repeated claim . . . is that most new jobs are created by small businesses . . . However, our main finding is that once we control for firm age there is no systematic relationship between firm size and growth. Our findings highlight the important role of business startups and young businesses in U.S. job creation. Business startups contribute substantially to both gross and net job creation.[20]

Similarly, another 2010 study from the Kauffman Foundation "shows that without startups, there would be no net job growth in the U.S. economy. This fact is true on average, but also is true for all but seven years for which the United States has data, going back to 1977." The report concludes:

---

20   Haltiwanger, John C., Ron S. Jarmin, Javier Miranda: NBER Working Paper 16300. "Who Creates Jobs? Small vs. Large vs. Young." August 2010.

All other ages of firms, including companies in their first full years of existence up to firms established two centuries ago, are net job destroyers . . . in terms of the life cycle of job growth, policymakers should appreciate the astoundingly large effect of job creation in the first year of a firm's life.[21]

The evidence of the job creation power of start-ups is right in front of our eyes and those of our policy makers. The implication is that government should be doing all it can to incentivize start-ups, as opposed to spending billions on subsidies and bailouts for existing large firms that, in the end, will not lead to one net American job. As summarized recently by Harvard Business School Professor Bill George:

Many of the great job creators of the past 25 years are companies that were barely visible in 1980 or even nonexistent: Target, Home Depot, Starbucks and Amazon in the retail field; Apple, Intel, Microsoft, Dell, Google, Oracle and Cisco Systems in information technology; and Genentech, Amgen, Stryker and Medtronic in medical technology. All of them were founded by entrepreneurs and are run by innovative leaders. Their ingenuity created the jobs boom in those years and enabled them to dominate global markets for their products.[22]

Moreover, the direct employment generated by companies like this doesn't measure their full impact. For example, Apple directly employs thousands of Americans. In addition, it indirectly creates job opportunities for many more, with hundreds of thousands of unique iPhone, iPod, and iPad, applications created outside Apple.

21 Kane, Tim. "The Importance of Startups in Job Creation and Job Destruction." *The Kauffman Foundation*. July 2010.

22 George, Bill. "Another View: Innovation Can Unlock Job Growth." *The New York Times*. December 1, 2009.

More, large U.S. companies spend an average of $3 billion on services from small companies, according to a 2010 study by the Business Roundtable.

So the more complete story of job creation is that large companies, smaller businesses, and business start-ups are each an important generator of jobs, and innovative start-ups in particular are the most powerful generators. These start-ups are built by entrepreneurs who have a better idea, the courage to take calculated risks, the ability to build a great team, and the leadership to build a great company. Entrepreneurs, even those who may fail, even many times, are a rare breed and a national treasure. For our economic future, our national policies must encourage and even celebrate entrepreneurship and innovation.

But tragically, business leaders in this country are all too often demonized by politicians and the media, who also proclaim that the government can create jobs. This mind-set, along with government actions inconsistent with business creation, are hurting our entrepreneurial lead in the world.

This isn't just my opinion. In September 2010, the Small Business Association (SBA) published a major study that examined thirty-one factors affecting entrepreneurship in seventy-one countries around the globe.[23] It found that the U.S. ranked third highest (behind Denmark and Canada). Although the SBA said that America's performance remained "strong," it issued a warning:

> The United States' apparent weakness in the tech sector and its lack of cultural support for entrepreneurship, coupled with lack of high-growth business, can be traced to a number of sources. Chief among these are the changing political environment and international volatility, the bursting of the tech sector bubble of the 1990s, the recent recession, and the improving performance of other countries.

---

23   Acs, Zoltan and Szerb, Laszlo. "Global Entrepreneurship and the United States." Small Business Administration. September 2010.

Most alarmingly, the SBA found that the reality of America's place "as a land of opportunity and as the Mecca for individuals wanting to do something new and different seems to be somewhat challenged by the facts." In particular, the report found:

> Cultural support for entrepreneurship and the American youth's perception of entrepreneurship as a viable career choice seem to be limited. Firms' performance in terms of growth and employment generation is not as strong, and the tech sector—the beacon of recent U.S. entrepreneurial success—is seen to have a lower score than the sample averages.

Similarly, a new book examining the Israeli economic miracle found that it has the world's highest density of technology-driven start-ups. Further, Israeli start-ups captured more venture capital investment per capita than any other country: "2.5 times the U.S., 30 times Europe, 80 times India, and 300 times China."[24] The authors specifically attribute this performance to an Israeli culture that fosters entrepreneurship and innovation.

INNOVATION-FRIENDLY NATIONAL POLICIES

Earlier, in chapter 3, I expressed my firm belief that the factors responsible for American exceptionalism are the reason that the U.S. has been the world leader in innovation. It follows that our national policies should seek to preserve and strengthen those factors, and many specific policies would necessarily follow from such a strategy. My personal preferred guidelines for specific policies include the following:

---

24 Senor, Dan and Singer, Saul. *Start-Up Nation: The Story of Israel's Economic Miracle.* Twelve. 2009.

Stop penalizing investments in start-ups. Some twenty years ago, virtually all private venture capital funding was directed into U.S.-based companies, but now more than half of such funding flows to foreign firms. What changed? Our federal government enacted policies making it less favorable for investment, while other countries encouraged investments. Our corporate tax rates became the second highest among developed countries, diminishing the returns to investors. The Sarbanes-Oxley law imposed new costs on business. Exiting investments became more difficult as going public became less desirable. Sarbanes-Oxley imposes relatively large costs on small public companies. More, public companies are catnip for plaintiffs' lawyers seeing quick and lucrative returns after any sudden change in share price. To encourage new investment, we need to modify Sarbanes-Oxley, restore integrity and rationality in our legal system, and lower corporate tax rates.

Direct any public funding of start-ups by private investors, not by government bureaucrats. Government employees generally are not at all qualified to make risky business investment decisions. Moreover, as shown in the failed 2009 stimulus package, government decisions invariably direct spending based on political impact criteria. I do not advocate any government spending of this type, but if politicians require taxpayer funding of start-ups, all specific investment decisions should be made by private venture capitalists with proven track records who would be required to share in the investment, risks, and rewards of their decisions. Government at most might prescribe targeted technologies. Interestingly, Josh Lerner, another Harvard business professor, argues that even government programs to stimulate bank lending are not relevant to start-ups, because entrepreneurial ventures cannot afford the financial burden of paying interest on loans.

Take easy unionization off the entrepreneurial table. As risk takers, entrepreneurs must have the ability to make fast decisions about what their companies do and how they do it. Unions inherently slow down and often inhibit fast action. This is exacerbated by proposals such as "card check" that allow sudden unionization without confidential balloting and that allow government arbitrators to set working conditions as well as work rules that drive entrepreneurs to seek more business-friendly host countries and take potential jobs with them. The Obama Administration's policies requiring unionized or "prevailing wage" government contractors add costs and reduce business incentives for struggling entrepreneurs. Closing off large government contracts to entrepreneurs would have had dire consequences in most of the wars the U.S. has fought.

Regrettably, until unions recognize that workers' interests, as with the nation's interests, lie with greater innovation and entrepreneurship, they represent a formidable barrier to those goals.

Let any company fail, whether large, small, or entrepreneurial. At its best, the free enterprise system is impartially rational in allocating investment, rewarding smart innovation, and promoting economic growth and job creation. Unfortunately, when political calculations intrude, outcomes are usually disastrous. The most recent major examples are the financial bailouts of GM and Chrysler, which not only wasted billions in taxpayer funds but were primarily motivated by an unprecedented gift to the pro-administration unions which suddenly were lifted ahead of the line of private creditors.

Billions of dollars in debt, Ford is further burdened by competing against Chrysler and GM, especially since the government wiped out their massive debts. This means Ford must pay several hundred million dollars in annual interest on its debt, while GM and Chrysler have little reason to invest.

Despite this, Ford stands as one of the most innovative and transformational companies of our era. It has shifted from a car company to a technology company. With a Ford F-150, a small business owner working construction can use an onboard computer, track tools, maintain supplies, and build efficiently.

Ford is one company that has not only innovated; it has also captured America's sense of fairness. Many Americans, disgusted at the car bailouts but wanting to buy an American company car, have turned to Ford and are thrilled by what they see.

For this reason, we have eagerly invited Ford CEO Alan Mulally to give the keynote address at International CES three times. Before Ford, Mulally headed Boeing, and many scoffed when a non-car executive was chosen to lead Ford. A board's selection of a CEO is its most important task, and the Ford Board proved innovative by thinking outside the Detroit box. Mulally is not only an affable and articulate leader, but his vision for Ford, his refusal to seek a bailout, and his shift of Ford to a technology company have proved to be a winning strategy. By the summer 2010, Ford revenues were up 30 percent from the same period a year ago.[25]

Another less-noticed consequence of the GM and Chrysler bailout was the unprecedented executive branch intervention into the process of bankruptcy and creditor rights. It may seem inconsequential, but those who lent Chrysler and General Motors billions of dollars, secured by a claim on the U.S. assets, were thrown overboard in favor of unions who essentially

---

25   Muller, Joann. "Ford Is Slowly Climbing Out of Debt." *Forbes.com.* July 23, 2010.

took ownership of these companies thanks to the Obama Administration's intervention. Nothing in the law gave the unions a more senior claim, but the White House intervention rushed through a bankruptcy reorganization, which gave the union rights and ownership over bondholders that had no principled basis in law and instead reeked of political payback for union support.

There is seldom a good reason for government preventing a business failure, and the default policy should be to let the free market work its will.

Make economics, business, and entrepreneurism studies compulsory in school curricula. At one time, reading, writing, and arithmetic marked the education of our populace. Over time, we added valuable requirements in subjects like history and geography. But over the last several decades, the education pendulum has swung toward subjects that have a tenuous relationship to good education and citizenship. As long as taxpayers are funding education at any level, we must educate our future generations about the true nature of their economic futures. They need to learn that private business, fact-based investing, innovation, and entrepreneurism will determine their own standards of living and the economic and political health of our country. Illiteracy in basic economics and entrepreneurism is a certain recipe for national failure.

Ensure that business tax rates are transparent and predictable. Uncertainty paralyzes decision-making in every realm of human activity. In our current political environment, business tax rates are being driven by ideological, not economically rational, considerations. As a result, entrepreneurs, their potential investors, and their potential customers all hesitate to make commitments. Although I hate to say so, even assured and measurable increases in marginal tax rates can be preferable compare to total uncertainty. It is another penalty that we suffer from when politics and ideology are directing our national policies.

Change tax laws to favor investment over debt. Our nation has been hurt as existing businesses employing millions of Americans have been bought and decimated by leveraged investment fund firms. These firms borrow heavily to purchase the going concerns, taking advantage of favorable income-tax-deductibility treatment of debt, and so turn a quick profit by firing workers, siphoning cash from the company, and letting it go under or trying to resell it quickly. A shift away from the tax advantage for debt would end many of these corporate dismemberments and job killers, and potentially promote additional investment for growth. If tax laws cannot be changed to favor investment, they should at minimum be neutral between them.

In sum, privately funded, entrepreneurial, technology-driven companies are the key to our nation's economic growth, increased standard of living, and full employment. Government never has been and never will be capable of rationally growing our economy and jobs. Its primary role should be to promote policies that enable the private sector to prosper and realize our ever-changing economic potential. I don't believe in censorship, but I am tempted to forbid the falsehood that government can ever create any jobs other than government jobs.

Moreover, government is also inherently driven by short-term, temporary, economic band aids. Just recently, former business school dean and Secretary of Labor and State George Schultz was joined by an elite group of scholars to critique the economically destructive tax-and-spending policies of the federal government. Among their wise policy recommendations, they point out that "long-lasting economic policies based on a long-term strategy work; temporary policies don't."[26] I heartily endorse their opinions.

---

26   Schultz, George, et al. "Principles for Economic Revival." *Wall Street Journal.* Sept. 16, 2010.

5

Innovation Requires Immigration

FOREIGN-BORN INNOVATORS

In 1979, a Russian family from Moscow immigrated to the United States. That might not seem like much today, with the collapse of the Soviet Union, but put yourself in this family's shoes. They were leaving behind one superpower for another superpower. But the strength of their native land was an illusion, as is so often the case with totalitarian regimes. The Soviet economy—and in turn its military might—was based on the sinister idea that the individual is nothing more than a tool of the state, another set of working hands that must do what a select few government bureaucrats told the individual to do. His or her dreams and talents didn't matter because he or she couldn't act on them anyway. All that mattered was the state and its single-minded attempt to govern every action of its citizens.

The father of this family, Michael, had wanted to be an astronomer, but the Communist Party, unofficially, barred Jews from studying physics because it didn't trust them with nuclear rocket research. He became a mathematician instead. Then, during a math conference in Warsaw, Michael had a chance to meet colleagues from the United States and Western European nations. That was the breaking point, as recounted by journalist Mark Malseed in a 2007 article in the magazine *Moment*.[27] "He said he wouldn't stay, now that he had seen what life could be about," recounted his wife.

Michael finally understood the ruse, as most behind the Iron Curtain did by the late 1970s. The "enemy," the United States, was their only chance to lead the life they wanted, to be free to do what they wanted. The flow of information from the Free World—the result of advances in innovation—gave the lie to the Communists' highly complex propaganda machine. This family knew what was waiting for them in America, and it wasn't what they had been told all their lives.

It was opportunity.

Michael and his family were granted permission to leave the Soviet Union. Going with them was Michael's six-year-old son, Sergey. Years later, Malseed reports, Sergey returned to his native land with his father, who was leading a two-week exchange program for his math students. Malseed writes:

> On the second day of the trip, while the group toured a sanitarium in the countryside near Moscow, Sergey took his father aside, looked him in the eye and said, "Thank you for taking us all out of Russia."

As his father had eleven years earlier, seventeen-year-old Sergey finally understood the ruse.

It's a touching story, and not at all unique in the short history of the United States. I'm glad I came across it while researching this chapter on immigration, too. You know how I found it? I Googled, of course. Or you could say I found it by using the very search engine Sergey Brin, along with his colleague Larry Page, invented in 1996, and which stands as one of the most consequential

---

27   Malseed, Mark. "The Story of Sergey Brin: 'How the Moscow-born Entrepreneur Found Google and Changed the Way the World Searches.'" *Moment*. February 2007.

innovations in our time. Nice work, Communists. You could have had Google first.

Instead, Google is an American innovation because we accepted the Brins into the country so that they could find a better life. But neither is Sergey Brin, for all his success, at all unique. We also accepted Intel founder Andy Grove (Hungary), eBay founder Pierre Omidyar (France), and Yahoo! founder Jerry Yang (Taiwan). The list goes on. There are the well-known: Alexander Graham Bell (Scotland); and the not-so-well-known: Emile Berliner (Germany), inventor of the phonograph.

Which leads to the obvious question: Where would America be without these foreign-born innovators? What would America's economy even look like?

It's a scary thought when you consider the "what-ifs." What if the United States had denied the Brins entry because they were from the Soviet Union—an avowed enemy of the United States? The simple fact is that immigrants are an instrumental part of American innovation and economic growth.

It's easy enough to say that we are a nation of immigrants. Almost all Americans are immigrants or descended from immigrants. Native Americans are less than 1 percent of the population.

But that doesn't mean that the United States has always been a welcoming country. Indeed, there are several moments in our history where a nativist surge helped stoke an anti-immigrant backlash. It's also true that each wave of immigrants—Irish, Germans, Italians, Eastern Europeans, Asians—has confronted bigotry upon reaching our shores. So while we applaud ourselves for being an "immigrant nation," we often forget just how hard it was for many of our forefathers when they first arrived.

But that's part of the immigrant spirit, isn't it? They don't come here for the *guarantee* of a better life. They come here for the *opportunity* for a better life. And whatever bigotry or nativist reaction they find, they endure because, in the end, it's infinitely better than what they left behind. They believed in a better future for their children—and almost all of them suffered so their children could have it better.

My wife's parents are great examples. They were trained as doctors in Communist Poland. In 1969, they escaped Poland to come to the United States with their then-five-year-old daughter (my future wife) to give her a better life. Penniless, they settled in the slums of Detroit. They had to learn English and retake their medical certification tests. They struggled for years but succeeded as physicians. Their daughter was valedictorian of her high school and now practices medicine as a talented retina surgeon, developing and implementing procedures that restore vision. (She's also a wonderful wife and mother.)

Clearly, my life is better off because they settled here. But so is our nation. You will find no more patriotic Americans than my wife and her parents. Indeed, my experience has been that almost all immigrants, from the innovators to the professionals to the cab drivers, are extremely patriotic and appreciative of what a gift it is to live here.

But maybe it is we who should be thanking them. Foreign-born innovators represent a substantial portion of the American economy. A 1999 University of California, Berkeley study found that Chinese and Indian engineers ran 24 percent of U.S. technology businesses started between 1980 and 1998. Following this study, the Kauffman Foundation investigated the matter further. In 2009, they released their results:

> We found that the trend [the UCB study] documented had become a nationwide phenomenon. According to the studies, in a quarter of the U.S. science and technology companies founded from 1995 to 2005, the chief executive or lead technologist was foreign-born.

In 2005, these companies generated $52 billion in revenue and employed 450,000 workers. In some industries, the numbers were much higher; in Silicon Valley, the percentage of immigrant-founded startups had increased to 52 percent. Indian immigrants founded 26 percent of these startups—more than the next four groups from Britain, China, Taiwan, and Japan combined.

These immigrant founders tended to be highly educated—96 percent held bachelor's degrees and 74 percent held graduate or postgraduate degrees, with 75 percent of these degrees in science, technology, engineering, and mathematics-related fields. The vast majority of these company founders didn't come to the United States as entrepreneurs—52 percent came to study, 40 percent came to work, and 5.5 percent came for family reasons. Only 1.6 percent came to start companies in America.

Even though these founders immigrated for other purposes initially, they typically started their companies just 13.25 years after arriving in the United States. And, rather than settling in well-established immigrant gateways, such as New York or Los Angeles, they moved to a diverse group of tech centers across the country and helped fuel their growth.[28]

Although remarkable, these results are not surprising. During the last half of the twentieth century, almost every top student in the world wanted to study and settle in America. This created an enormous American talent pool of the best and the brightest. In the 1990s, when I would meet with my counterparts who also ran technology associations around the world, they would complain that the United States was taking their smartest students.

---

28   Wadhwa, Vivek. "Foreign-Born Entrepreneur: An Underestimated American Resource." *Kauffman Thoughtbook*. 2009. 177–181.

RISK-TAKERS

We can say that the success rate of highly motivated immigrants is a result of the U.S. economic system, which encourages risk and rewards success. But I think this only tells half the story. The other half is on account of the immigrants themselves, who, like Sergey Brin's father, risked everything to build a better life.

In other words, the type of people who choose to immigrate to the United States is just as important as the economic system they find when landing here. These are the risk-takers of the world. It takes a certain person to leave everything he or she knows behind to come to a strange new land. But that's just the type of people who have always come here.

From the founders of our country onward, the pioneering spirit that leads the world is a product of our immigrant background. The early European settlers left behind religious persecution and government tyranny to create their own societies, the frontiersmen of the early Republic carved out a nation from a wilderness, and today industries like Silicon Valley are on the cutting edge of discovering what's possible. Like the results of the Kauffman Foundation study, none of this is a coincidence.

This land of opportunity attracts not only the best and the brightest—but also the risk takers who want something better for their children. Our nation is the most diverse in the world. Our national gene pool includes those who hungered for something better and instilled that desire genetically and spiritually in their children. As AnnaLee Saxenian, author of the original 1999 Berkeley study, said in a 2007 interview:

> The advantage of entrepreneurs is that they're generally creating new opportunities and new wealth that didn't even exist before them. Just by leaving your home country, you're taking a risk, and

that means you're willing to take risks in business. You put them in an environment that supports entrepreneurship, and this is the logical outcome.[29]

But an immigrant's ability to add his or her ingenuity to the U.S. economy—creating wealth and jobs—rests on two very important factors: 1.) Do we let him or her in? and 2.) Do we let him or her stay here? Let's return to the Kauffman Foundation study:

We found that, as of September 30, 2006, 500,040 individuals in the main employment-based visa categories and an additional 555,044 family members were in line for permanent-resident status in the United States. Another 126,421—who already had job offers—were waiting abroad, a total of 1,181,505 educated and skilled professionals waiting to gain legal permanent-resident status.

Thus, far more skilled workers are waiting for U.S. visas than can be admitted under current law. Only around 120,000 visas are available for skilled immigrants in the key employment categories. These numbers are particularly troubling when you consider that no more than 7 percent of the visas may be allocated to immigrants from any one country. So, immigrants from countries with large populations like India and China have the same number of visas available (8,400) as those from Iceland and Mongolia. We estimate that more than one-third of the million workers in line for permanent resident visas are from India.

This means that immigrants from the most populous countries who file for permanent resident visas today could be waiting indefinitely. In the meantime, they can't start companies or lay deep roots in American society.

---

29   Konrad, Rachel. "Immigrants Behind 25 Percent of Tech Startups." *MSNBC*. January 3, 2007.

Indeed, the Kauffman study further notes that there's been an influx in the number of foreign nationals filing U.S. patent applications (337 percent over eight years, to be exact):

> In 2006, foreign nationals residing in the United States were named as inventors or co-inventors in an astounding 25.6 percent of patent applications filed from the United States, a substantial increase from 7.6 percent in 1998. Foreign nationals also contributed to a majority of some U.S. companies' patent applications, including Qualcomm—72 percent, Merck—65 percent, GE—64 percent, and Cisco—60 percent. More than 40 percent of the U.S. government-filed international patent applications had foreign authors.

These foreign nationals were doing business within the United States, working alongside American companies, but they weren't allowed to become Americans. And when they can't get in, the fruit of their ingenuity and labor goes elsewhere.

But if they're doing business in the United States, adding to our companies' growth, then why does it matter? Because we need these innovative foreign nationals to build their lives in the United States, not simply contribute every once in a while. The immigrants go where the opportunity is, and if they can't set down roots and build a life, they will move on, taking all that wonderful immigrant spirit with them.

I can't say it better than the Kauffman study, so let's return to it one last time:

> We are on the verge of a reverse "brain-drain." If the United States doesn't fix its policies and keep these highly skilled immigrants, India and China will welcome them home. So will countries like Singapore, Canada, Dubai, and Australia, which are opening their arms to skilled immigrants. They will start their ventures in Bangalore

or Shanghai instead of Silicon Valley and Research Triangle Park. Our loss will be their gain.

After September 11, 2001, we flipped a switch and began discouraging this brain fuel for our economy. We pulled back the welcome mat and put up real and perceived barriers to the world's educated people who previously would have studied or created companies in America. Today, other nations welcome these students, entrepreneurs, and engineers. Our recent reputation for unfriendliness creates an impression of xenophobia and increasingly repels the best and the brightest. This is not only a shame, but it is also harmful to our future.

As a recent Small Business Administration report notes:

A direct impact of 9/11 has been felt in the tightening of U.S. immigration policy. Though required due to security concerns and rising domestic opposition to illegal immigration, it has nevertheless affected entrepreneurship in the United States to some extent by controlling the flow of skilled workers into the country. In this respect, countries like Canada, New Zealand, and Australia have all been more pragmatic by giving strong incentives to attract educated, skilled workers to their shores—whether doctors, engineers, or academic researchers—and to keep them there with offers of residency and citizenships. Accompanying a tighter U.S. immigration policy is a growing feeling of disenchantment among large sections of the American population, including the existing immigrant groups, who are at times limited and constrained in terms of opportunities to exploit their potential and skills.[30]

---

30   Acs, Zoltan and Szerb, Laszlo. "Global Entrepreneurship and the United States." Small Business Administration. September 2010.

We must reverse course and work to attract these future entrepreneurs. Even if we start modestly, just at the university level, we are creating ambassadors of goodwill when they leave. But if we are strategic, we will insist that they stay, even after they get their degree. More than half of the 22,500 doctorates in science and engineering awarded by U.S. universities in 2007 went to foreign nationals.

Why would we not immediately offer a PhD student citizenship? Because he or she is from a nation that harbors terrorists? Do a background check. Because we've filled our quota from his or her country for the year? A doctorate should be an exception to the quota.

Denying citizenship to our top university students is an insane policy if the United States wants to keep pace with the rest of the developing world. Most countires gladly take the engineers we don't want. Moreover, if we care about our competitiveness, we will expand the H1B visa program and get the highly skilled talent here rather than forcing our companies to locate their facilities elsewhere in the world.

According to a recent National Science Foundation report, of 568,000 foreign students who studied in the United States in 2008, 248,000 were enrolled in science and engineering fields. The second highest field in terms of enrollment was business, with 120,000 students.[31]

These numbers should drive home the point that it's no secret why students come to the United States to study: They come because we offer the best science and engineering education in the world. But once here, why would we then send them back home? Why wouldn't we let them use what we've taught them to build wealth and jobs in America?

Our best hope for economic growth is immigration. According

---

31   Burrelli, Joan. "Foreign Science and Engineering Students in the United States." *National Science Foundation*. July 2010.

to a 2008 Future of Small Business report by Intuit Inc., immigrants have higher rates of starting a new business than native-born Americans. Remarkably, immigrant men start businesses at a rate that is 71 percent higher than native-born men, while immigrant women are starting businesses at a rate 57 percent higher than native-born women.[32]

The report notes:

> Through small business formation, the growth of the U.S. immigrant pool is driving economic growth and success in a number of major U.S. cities. In the "Los Angeles Economy Project," the Milken Institute reports that the economic recovery of Los Angeles is due in part to immigrants forming new businesses. The local economy is becoming global as immigrants and others use cross-national market knowledge and ties to develop their businesses.

In addition to the entrepreneurs, we also need the diligent, motivated, hard-working immigrants who did not have the opportunity to receive advanced degrees. A subject of intense controversy today, this group takes the jobs Americans don't want, even in an economic downturn. Most of them also pay taxes and appreciate what this nation has to offer. Yes, some of them are illegal, but they don't need to be.

INCREASING THE RIGHT KIND OF IMMIGRATION

Proposals on increasing immigration may be the most counter-intuitive, and among the least popular in the national debate today. Both union liberals and conservative right-wingers agree

---

32 "Intuit 2020 Report: 'Twenty Trends That Will Shape The Next Decade'." *Intuit.com.* October 2010.

that immigration should be limited, even reversed in some cases, because they claim that immigrants are taking jobs from Americans and driving up costs, such as health care. As these two factions are usually also the biggest campaign donors, they have the ear of many politicians.

One of the most difficult and frankly frustrating discussions I've had took place on the air on CNN when I debated Lou Dobbs on his eponymous program. Although styled as a news hour, it was really just a platform given to Dobbs by Time Warner to broadcast an anti-immigrant screed each night. Dobbs played on blue-collar fears of immigrants stealing their jobs. Such xenophobia led Dobbs to argue that closing our borders was the only way to save our economy. This position runs counter to the fact that 95 percent of the world's consumers live outside of the U.S. and purchase billions of dollars of American-made products each year.

But the unavoidable truth is that a growth economy requires an expanding population, and the immigrants are the hardest working, most entrepreneurial, and hungriest for success in our society. What the extremes of either wing don't want to admit is that denying our nation this vital work force is a recipe for long-term economic decline. With that in mind, there are specific actions we should take.

Enable visas and citizenship for bright and gifted students. We should want the world's best and brightest to come here. We need to change our visa programs to make it easy for them and to show them they are welcome. Not only should we change the policy that makes all foreign nations the same in terms of visa quotas, but we should also create a separate visa category for bright students and gifted people to get visas. More, we need to let the best and most promising university students stay in the country once they receive their degrees. A university degree should represent a path to citizenship in the United States.

Allow a quick path to citizenship for entrepreneurs and the financially able. We want the world's most savvy and innovative people. We want people who can invest and start new businesses. We can create criteria and thresholds for acceptability (e.g., English proficiency, no criminal record, references, etc.), but we need to put out the welcome mat for them. Canada opens its doors to any person who has a net worth of $300,000. I'm not suggesting that wealthy immigrants purchase their visas or citizenships, but I am saying that a portion of our immigration policy should function like a venture capitalist meeting: If we see promise, we should want to invest.

Create criteria and a process for granting citizenship to qualified immigrants. We want to attract immigrants who will work hard, contribute to our society, learn English, and respect our laws. This means careful screening and even visas prior to citizenship. Every immigrant who wants to stay and become a citizen should be screened. This does not require a big new bureaucracy, but rather empowering American citizens, who could volunteer to sit on committees that determine who should be allowed the privilege of citizenship. Immigrants would apply to these citizenship boards, which would have a degree of oversight and rules applied to them to prevent fraud and abuse. But an immigrant should be allowed to make his or her case.

Resolve other immigration problems quickly. Our nation is challenged by a large group of people who came here illegally seeking a better life. Some believe this group costs us much more than it can collectively contribute. Others see hardworking people contributing to our society. Both sides are passionate, both sides have valid points, but the hostility of each side to the other has prevented Washington from reaching a solution to our immigration problems. We need to resolve the problem, quickly. The sooner we do, the sooner we can start the business of returning America to the land of opportunity to the world's best and brightest.

These individuals did come here illegally, and they impose costs. But they also are generally hard-working and do the dirtiest work in society. Even with our high unemployment, Americans do not line up for these jobs. If illegal immigrants were sent home tomorrow, it would impose huge costs on our nation. If we make them citizens, we are encouraging law-breaking. In any event, we need to agree that any new citizens from this group establish a proficiency in English, show an ability to hold a job, and have some way of ensuring contrition if there is to be a path to citizenship. We must also put an end to our porous borders. As hard-working as some of these immigrants are, a nation that cannot maintain the integrity of its borders will not be a nation for long.

Don't allow entry of all relatives of all citizens. As to other new immigrants, we need to examine the free entry for all relatives. I suggest that we limit entry to blood relatives and spouses of U.S. citizens with financial ability (e.g., pay $20,000 for each immigrant), and that the host relatives be taxpaying citizens. Moreover, we need to assess the practicality of immediate citizenship granted to everyone born in our physical borders. This is now unique to our nation, and it creates perverse incentives for illegal immigration of parents-to-be.

Make English our official language. Supporting immigration does not mean lessening America. I am amazed that we have not made English our official language. It is not insensitivity to require those who would enjoy the benefits of this nation to learn the customs of this nation. We should not have to "press 1 for English." If we want immigrants to succeed in this country, having them learn English as a requirement for citizenship will quickly assimilate them into American society.

Our politicians must set aside their demagogic appeals to the electorate for short-term gain and realize the destruction they're causing to our innovation industry. America is what it is because of our immigration heritage. Without it we will lose our creative fire.

6

The U.S. Constitution
and the Fire of Genius

"Next came the Patent laws. These began in England in 1624; and, in this country, with the adoption of our Constitution. Before then, any man might instantly use what another had invented; so that the inventor had no special advantage from his own invention. The patent system changed this; secured to the inventor, for a limited time, the exclusive use of his invention; *and thereby added the fuel of interest to the fire of genius, in the discovery and production of new and useful things.*"

—ABRAHAM LINCOLN, Second Lecture on Discoveries and Inventions,
February 11, 1859

PATENTS

The only U.S. president to hold a patent is Abraham Lincoln. In 1848, in between sessions of Congress, Lincoln was on his way home to Illinois when his boat became stuck on a sandbar. As his law partner, William Herndon, would later recount in his biography of Lincoln:

> The captain ordered the hands to collect all the loose planks, empty barrels and boxes and force them under the sides of the boat. These

empty casks were used to buoy it up. After forcing enough of them under the vessel she lifted gradually and at last swung clear of the opposing sand bar . . . Lincoln had watched this operation very intently . . . Continual thinking on the subject of lifting vessels over sand bars and other obstructions in the water suggested to him the idea of inventing an apparatus for this purpose.

This episode led Lincoln to design a device to lift boats over shoals, and in 1849 he managed to obtain Patent No. 6469. Whatever the merits behind Herndon's observation that the device was "impractical," Lincoln's patent was never put into use and his flotation device never manufactured—perhaps fortunately for the state of the union.

But Lincoln's appreciation for innovation remained with him all his life. Ten years later, he would deliver an address on "Discoveries and Inventions" (quoted above), in which he heralded not only human ingenuity but also, and perhaps for the emerging politician more importantly, the legal framework protecting innovators. Lincoln observed that the innovation of the *theory* behind patents provided the necessary "fuel of interest" to entice a person to pursue technological innovation ("fire of genius").

Of course Americans didn't invent the idea of patents, nor was Lincoln the first American president to recognize the importance of legal protections for innovators. The idea went as far back as the Middle Ages. Also, at the time of the founding, Great Britain had extensive experience with patent laws, and these formed the basis for the fledgling states' own patent laws before the Constitutional Convention.

But the United States was the first to enshrine what eventually became known as the Copyright Clause in a founding document. Although the British had the Statute of Anne, the first statute to protect copyrights, the United States actually put in our Constitution Article 1, Section 8, Clause 8: "To promote the Progress of Science and useful Arts, by securing for limited Times to Authors and Inventors the exclusive Right to their respective Writings and Discoveries."

To the men in Philadelphia, the matter of whether to include patent law was never questioned, at least insofar as the record provides. The clause passed unanimously, as written, and it's not difficult to see why. The world was just beginning to change in dramatic ways. England, though the enemy, was still looked at with admiration for its law codes and industrial progress. Exciting things were happening in England, and the forward-thinking Americans wanted a part of it.

Men like Benjamin Franklin and Thomas Jefferson, innovators themselves, and George Washington believed much of the young nation's future depended on whether it could match Europe's technological prowess. Until that occurred, Jefferson knew the United States had to rely on the European innovation. In 1821 he wrote, "In an infant country like ours we must much depend for improvement on the science of other countries, longer established, possessing better means, and more advanced than we are."

Indeed, Jefferson himself, while Secretary of State, served as the nation's first patent commissioner and patent examiner—there was no Patent Office at the time—and approved the first U.S. patent in 1790 to one Samuel Hopkins for an improvement in the making of potash.

In President Washington's first address to Congress, he said, "I cannot forbear intimating to you the expediency of giving effectual encouragement, as well to the introduction of new and useful inventions from abroad as to the exertion of skill and genius at home." In other words, let's get innovating, Congress.

But despite the centrality of patent law—and the notion of intellectual property rights—in the founding of our country, there have always been challenges. Eli Whitney, for instance, and his cotton gin (patented in 1794) revolutionized the cotton industry. Today, were someone to invent a machine of equal importance, that person would be rich beyond his wildest dreams. But Whitney barely made a dime because other farmers merely copied his design. Whitney sued and spent whatever profits he had made on legal fees, before going out of business in 1797.

Nevertheless, the founders had a vision of a nation where the government had a limited role in commerce but a significant role in protecting intellectual property. In fact, James Madison wanted to give rewards to innovators. The founders never tired of trying to get it right. The Patent Act of 1790 was replaced by the Patent Act of 1793, which in time was replaced by the Patent Act of 1836.[33] As the nation grew, so did the number of innovators, whose filings kept revealing flaws in the current system. We don't need to go through all the history of the Patent Office here. Needless to say, the founders' vision of inducing American innovation seemed to be working.

But if the Constitution provided the framework protecting innovators, it was the Bill of Rights that created an atmosphere in which innovation could thrive. What if the VCR, the Internet, and computers had been banned in the United States because they allowed duplication of copyrighted content?

The First Amendment to the U.S. Constitution protects freedom of speech. Our founders did not know of movies or the Internet, obviously, but they were prescient. They were very much aware of the importance and power of the press, and the innovation of the printing press wasn't so long ago that it was ancient history in the late eighteenth century.

THE FIRST AMENDMENT AND INNOVATION

The First Amendment is not only a broad legal protection; it is also the charter for our unique questioning culture. It molded our

---

33   Of course, successor laws improved the patent system.

nation's spirit of encouraging creativity and individual expression. The colonial pamphleteers, such as Thomas Paine and Samuel Adams, were today's bloggers—amateur journalists and activists whose influence extended far beyond their meager means.

Not that the founders weren't wary of a completely unfettered press—it had helped start and sustain a revolution, after all—but they weren't about to limit the very thing that they had fought England to defend.

By making the very first change to the Constitution an express right to challenge the status quo, the founders helped maintain more than two centuries of American success. Today this means that blogs, movies, podcasts, and scientific theories can be created and publically shared freely and without fear of government censorship.

Fortunately for us, despite efforts to restrict these products, our Constitution allowed these new forms of expression and content delivery to exist. If patent and copyright protection weren't necessarily American innovations, a free and independent press enshrined in a constitution certainly was.

Our diverse population has the legal and cultural capacity to express itself not only for political speech but for *any* reason. These not only encourage us to write and create, but they also protect our ability to share our creations on Facebook, YouTube, and on blogs.

Sometimes this innovation and creativity are for political purposes—surely sacred under the First Amendment. But often the views and the spirit of the First Amendment are what allow new businesses to be launched, such as Web sites like Craigslist or the Drudge Report.

If you think about how almost every successful new business or innovation challenges the status quo and creates competition, you realize that innovators need special protections. The First Amendment is an important protection in ensuring that innovators can try something new. It ensures that a government or existing business cannot shut down an innovator by fiat. It allows an innovator threatened by government to make a plea to the courts of law and of public opinion. It encourages a culture where innovation can flourish.

The First Amendment has played a real but unheralded role in our national innovation strategy. It is our "special sauce." It is easier to be creative when there is no fear of jail time for violating some censor or authority figure.

However, in America, the danger to innovation usually comes from the private sector, not government. Representing the technology industry, I often confront established industries threatened by innovation. These battles are fought over that No Man's Land between copyright law and the First Amendment.

I recounted my experience in the VCR wars in chapter 2, but there was more at stake than whether a consumer could record his favorite television shows. As the controversy grew, the music industry joined the side of the movie industry in trying to restrict and put royalties (or taxes) on recording technology.

The music industry had a long history of opposing new innovation and of lobbying Congress to squelch competing technologies. Copyright law had evolved so that composers and performers as well as the record companies were paid through "compulsory licenses" (some would say taxes) on "talking" pictures, the jukebox, the player piano, and various other music services. Other than their inability to get radio stations to pay a fee to record companies and their artists, the music industry has had an excellent history of getting Congress to step in and do its bidding.

So in 1982, when the motion picture industry started to get traction in Congress against the VCR, the music industry saw an opportunity to once again exploit the situation. And it was initially successful. Soon legislation was introduced that would put royalty taxes on all audio recording equipment and blank tape.

The timing was perfect. Although the nation was in a recession, a revolution in music listening was under way. In 1979, Sony introduced the Walkman, which completely changed the music industry because the Walkman allowed portable music. The CD was just being introduced as well, although we were a long way from portable CD players. (These were the bulky home stereo kind that cost a fortune.) But the music industry initially refused to produce quality pre-recorded cassettes or CDs. It wasn't solely for anti-innovation reasons either.

Years earlier, a spasm of excitement had similarly surrounded eight-track cassettes. The format was novel and initially popular, but it required a heavy investment from the record companies. When sales fell off, the recording companies were left holding the bag. They didn't want to get burned again by some new, flash-in-the-pan gadget like the Walkman.

The other reason was that the record labels didn't want to lose control of their music, which the technology behind the VCR and recordable cassette tapes threatened to do. So it allied with the movie industry and sought restrictions on the new products. We faced an alliance of two great American industries with legendary lobbies and tons of money. Not exactly what I would call adhering to the founders' spirit of innovation. (Then again, the founders did include the right to petition the government alongside freedom of speech in the First Amendment.)

And as I've already recounted, the innovators won the day at the Supreme Court in a 5–4 decision. But it still amazes me that if one justice had gone the other way we would be living in a different world. I am not sure what the world would be—but certainly it would have less innovation, less access to technology, and a different set of companies in control. Apple's iPod would not have been possible, nor would a host of other products we take for granted today. The digital revolution, which began in the late 1970s, would look quite different today, if it had happened at all.

But thankfully we'll never know what that alternate world would have looked like. The market was quickly validating the Supreme Court results. VCR prices were falling, and average Americans were buying VCRs and loving them. Hollywood may have lost in the Supreme Court, but its pre-recorded video cassette sales were growing and the innovation of the VCR—essentially creating personal movie theaters—greatly expanded the content industry as home movie-goers purchased or rented movies to watch at their leisure. Hollywood quickly adopted the new technology as its own.

The recording industry is another story. Although it eventually embraced CDs, its initial resistance to selling quality pre-recorded cassettes changed consumer behavior. Consumers responded by bypassing the major record labels and swapping cassettes with only the songs they wanted to hear—what the kids call "mixed tapes," which amazingly are already a thing of the past. Music lovers made the technology work for them by going around the record industry, and they grew accustomed to avoiding the industry all together. This helped create the singles-based music economy—which soon destroyed the album-based revenue gravy train.

The long, slow decline continues to this day, when consumers can purchase a single song on iTunes for 99 cents. When people think of music, they think of iTunes, iPods, and MP3 players—devices that allow them to customize their listening experience. Can your teenager name one major record company?

Despite the Supreme Court decision, our battles with the content industries, such as Hollywood and the recording industries, go on. The music industry succeeded in controlling CD rentals and restricting the unfettered recording ability of non-computer consumer electronics products. The result is that few of these products are sold, and the entire concept of music recording has shifted to the Internet.

But for the music industry, these are Pyrrhic victories. It has never been able to recover from its decision, made thirty years ago, to oppose innovation. The results are clear. Total revenue from music sales and licensing has fallen from $14.6 billion in 1999 to $6.3 billion in 2009. Music executives must look back on the late 1970s and early 1980s and ask themselves, "What were we thinking?" Perhaps the shift from albums to singles would have been avoided or delayed if the music industry had spent more time and money investing in new formats and less time asking Congress to restrict them.

But the music industry, along with other content industries, had their victories. Congress acted fourteen different times over the past fifty years to lengthen the copyright term. It is now roughly one hundred years. Ironically, the last extension was pushed by Disney, which has made billions of dollars using public domain stories like Snow White and the Hans Christian Andersen fairy tales.

Make no mistake; I'm not opposed to copyrights or patents. But I agree with Jefferson's denunciation of what he called "monopolies of invention," which is the jealous guarding of an innovation at the expense of further progress. In 1813, he wrote:

> [O]ther nations have thought these monopolies produce more embarrassment than advantage to society; and it may be observed that the nations which refuse monopolies of invention, are as fruitful as England in new and useful devices.[34]

A content provider naturally wants to own the content for as long as possible, much as a monopolist wants to maintain the monopoly for as long as possible. After all, monopolists are first and foremost capitalists. But where would the DVD player be today if Universal Studios had refused to produce its movies on VCR tapes? Would cell phones be as widespread today if cell phone makers banned

---

34 Matsuura, Jeffrey H. "Thomas Jefferson and the Evolution of a Populist Vision of Intellectual Property Rights and Democratic Values." *Archipelago.org*. November 3, 2006.

calling to competitors' phones? Certainly if patents did not exist we would have fewer innovations, but if they were more than five times their duration—like the 100 years of copyright—we would have less innovation building on prior innovation.

Limiting patent and copyrights certainly doesn't help the innovator, but it helps innovation. Building on originality is also innovation. Government-granted monopolies in copyrights or patents must neither be too long or too short. It's difficult for an innovator to give up rights to the product of his or her work. And yet that's the only way innovation can flourish.

The battles of the last thirty years have proven that to err on the side of technology is always good policy. Although we must always endure the painful disruptions innovation creates, we must never think that this is a good enough reason to ban progress.

And that's because innovation is so much more than a boon to economic growth. It breaks boundaries, it connects people from distant lands, it fires the imagination, and it sends a message of hope to those who most need it. In a word, innovation is freedom.

The VCR and fax machine helped bring down the Berlin Wall. Radio and videotapes helped collapse the Soviet Union. Millions behind the Iron Curtain were able to listen to American rock music and to hear Ronald Reagan speak to them of an "evil empire." And it continues to this day. The Internet is allowing millions of new businesses to be created in Africa and India. It reaches those in Communist China, which attempts to restrict access. Indeed it is no wonder that the most totalitarian and isolated countries in the world also most severely restrict access to technology.

When it comes to the Constitution, we don't need new policy suggestions for innovation; rather we need a recognition that it is because of the Constitution that we have the structure and incentive in this country to innovate. Although the founders could not foresee the world we live in today, they knew enough to know the tools we would need to thrive as an innovative nation, which are the same tools they used. The First Amendment and copyright law derive from our unique history, from our grounding in English law and our start as rabble-rousing revolutionaries spreading our subversive messages. It is our job to protect these twin tools of innovation in our own time, to oppose legislative attempts that give an industry or company unfair advantage, and to make sure our judicial branch upholds the original intent of the Constitution.

The ongoing conflict between copyright laws and our First Amendment will continue to wage. It is a testament to the system of innovation our founders created over 200 years ago, which they inherited from even older generations. Freedom of speech and copyright laws are both necessary for innovation. Both are necessary for the "fire of genius." And both should be embraced by society.

7

All the World's a Market: Innovation Requires Free Trade

Bloomberg, June 14, 2010

Canadian lawmakers today approved a free trade agreement with Colombia, a move that may give its agricultural producers an advantage over U.S. competitors in the Latin American country . . . "In adopting this free trade agreement, Canada will be in a very strong competitive position vis-à-vis our other competition around the world and this will mean a great deal to our agricultural sector," Canadian Trade Minister Peter Van Loan told reporters earlier today.

Colombian Trade Minister Luis Guillermo Plata said in an April 28 interview that Canadian exporters may gain as U.S. lawmakers delay approval of their free-trade agreement . . . "Many of the things that we buy from the U.S. we could buy from Canada and we could buy tariff-free," Plata, 42, said in the interview . . .

Prime Minister Stephen Harper's governing Conservatives have made strengthening ties with Latin America a priority in an effort to broaden markets for Canadian commodities and reduce the country's dependence on the U.S. economy.[35]

---

35   Argitis, Theophilos. "Canadian Lawmakers Approve Free Trade Agreement With Colombia." *Bloomberg.com*. June 14, 2010.

The Wall Street Journal, Sept. 17, 2010:

BRUSSELS—European governments Thursday approved a free trade agreement with South Korea, the world's 12th-largest economy. With bilateral trade at $74.3 billion last year, it is one of the biggest free trade deals ever between two economies . . . Starting [July 1, 2011], tariffs will be phased out on 96% of European and 99% of South Korean goods within three years. All levies on industrial goods will be eliminated within five years.

The deal is a coup for EU trade negotiators. The EU started talks with South Korea in 2007, the same year as the U.S. Fearing a protectionist backlash, however, the administration of U.S. President Barack Obama hasn't yet presented the U.S.–South Korea free trade agreement to Congress . . . According to EU estimates, the deal will generate an additional $25 billion of additional exports for EU producers. It will likely be in the high-technology industrial sectors where Europe is strong. Top EU exports to South Korea in 2009 were nuclear machinery and parts, $8.6 billion, electronics, $3.4 billion, and cars and trucks, $2 billion.

"The European Union is the world's No. 1 economic bloc and South Korea's second-largest trading partner," South Korea's Ministry of Foreign Affairs and Trade said in a statement. "The pact will bring about economic benefit more than a free trade pact signed with the U.S."[36]

FREE TRADE

In March 2010, President Obama announced plans to double U.S. exports in five years. "Those who once would oppose any trade agreement now understand that there are new markets and new

---

36   Dalton, Matthew and John W. Miller. "EU Nations Approve Free Trade Pact With South Korea." *The Wall Street Journal*. September 17, 2010.

sectors out there that we need to break into if we want our workers to get ahead," he said.[37] The president made a direct call on Congress to pass the pending free-trade agreements with Panama, Colombia, and South Korea, which have been stalled in Congress since Democrats took control in 2006.

In July 2010, President Obama announced the creation of an export-promotion council, chaired by Boeing Chief Executive James McNerney and Xerox CEO Ursula Burns. "Ninety-five percent of the world's customers and fastest-growing markets are beyond our borders. So if we want to find new growth streams, if we want to find new markets and new opportunity, we've got to compete for those new customers," the president said.[38]

In September 2010, the president's export-promotion council released a report recommending that the federal government expand its trade promotion efforts and finish work on the pending free-trade agreements. "The more American companies export, the more they produce. And the more they produce, the more people they hire, and that means more jobs—good jobs that often pay as much as 15 percent more than average."[39]

Although the agreements were entered into by President Bush years earlier, President Obama has been consistent in indicating he wanted them passed. Unfortunately, in doing nothing to move them, so has Congress. Almost a year after the president announced his export initiative, the free-trade agreements are still pending. Meanwhile, as the above news stories make abundantly clear, the rest of the world is not waiting on the United States to get its act together in opening new markets for American goods.

---

37   Schneider, Howard. "Obama's Ambitious Export Plan May Rekindle Free-trade Battle." *Washington Post*. March 12, 2010.

38   Sinai, Allen. "Cap Gains Taxation: Less Means More." *The Wall Street Journal*. September 21, 2010.

39   Goldman, Julianna and Nicholas Johnston. "Obama Turns Focus to Trade as Way to Encourage Economic Growth." *Bloomberg.com*. September 16, 2010.

Free trade is the conduit through which the world's citizens are able to improve their standard of living. Free trade lowers the costs of goods for everyone and opens markets where none before existed. In today's increasingly connected world, there is no justifiable reason a consumer can't get a product from anywhere in the world with the click of a mouse.

As it relates to innovation, free trade vastly expands the market opportunities for U.S. tech companies, adding to economic growth and jobs. At home, Americans get lower-cost consumer technologies that enable them to innovate and create new businesses, Web sites, and content. When the cost of doing business is lower, the cost of starting a business is lower.

According to the Commerce Department's Bureau of Economic Analysis, royalty and licensing fees paid to America's innovators from overseas is on pace to reach $100 billion in 2010. Between 2003 and 2008, royalty and licensing fees paid to Americans doubled from $48 billion to $93 billion annually.[40]

Also, exports in other intellectual property–intensive industries nearly doubled over the same period. Income from exports of IT-related services, such as research and development and computer and database services, rose from $17.7 billion to just under $30 billion. Exports of medicines and pharmaceuticals rose from just over $20 billion to just over $40 billion.

But as long as these trade agreements remain stalled, U.S. firms trying to sell to potential markets like Colombia face higher tariffs than our competition. In September, Colombia announced that its 2010 exports will reach $40 billion and that it expects sales to double in the next four years.[41] In addition to Canada,

---

40   United States. Office of the United States Intellectual Property Enforcement Coordinator. *Intellectual Property Spotlight.* August 2010.

41   Crowe, Darcy. "Colombia: Exports to Reach $40 Billion in '10; Double in 4 Years." *The Wall Street Journal.* September 8, 2010.

Colombia is also pursuing a trade deal with another U.S. competitor, Japan.

Moreover, Colombia's domestic consumer electronics market was estimated to be worth $3.3 billion in 2008, and it is expected to reach $5.1 billion by 2013.[42] These aren't insignificant numbers. They reflect a growing economy in an economically strategic part of the world. Yet the U.S. is willfully cutting itself off from entering this new market.

The rest of the world wants American dollars. They want us to buy their goods. But they will also not pass on the opportunity to form a free-trade bloc with other nations to get a competitive advantage over the United States. The EU is doing this right now, as are several East Asian nations. Americans now face two powerful spheres of free trade, one in the EU and the other in Asia. Our shift toward protectionism and toward walls around our country will lead to devastating consequences for our economy.

Inaction on trade deals is already costing American jobs. According to C. Fred Bergsten, director of the Peterson Institute for International Economics, every $1 billion in addition exports produces about 7,000 new jobs. Writing in the *Washington Post*, Bergsten notes that passing the Colombian and South Korean agreements could save around 300,000 American jobs.[43]

The Wall Street Journal story quoted earlier mentions that the EU–South Korean free-trade agreement will generate $25 billion in additional exports for EU producers. Talk about outsourcing. Keeping with Bergsten's formula, the EU should expect to generate roughly 175,000 jobs with its South Korean trade deal alone.

Meanwhile, a U.S Chamber of Commerce report found that the United States' existing free-trade agreements with fourteen

---

42   "Colombia Consumer Electronics Report." *Snipsly.com*. June 22, 2010.

43   Bergsten, C. Fred. "How Best to Boost U.S. Exports." *Washington Post*. February 3, 2010.

countries in 2008 generated $304.5 billion in output (or 2.1 percent of U.S. GDP), expanded total U.S. exports of goods and services to the world by $462.7 billion, and supported 5.4 million U.S. jobs.[44]

The Chamber of Commerce also looked at what effect the failure to implement the pending free-trade agreements has had on the U.S. economy. It found:

Specifically, failure to implement the U.S. FTAs while our trading partners go forward with their FTAs would lead to a decline of $40.2 billion in U.S. exports of goods and services and U.S. national output failing to grow by $44.8 billion. We estimate that the total net negative impact on U.S. employment from these trade and output losses could total 383,400.[45]

Now take the 1994 North American Free Trade Agreement (NAFTA). In a humorous but telling flip-flop, during the 2008 Democratic primary debate, candidate Barack Obama spoke out consistently against NAFTA, even attacking his opponent, then-Senator Hillary Clinton, for her supposed support of the trade agreement. But then word leaked that one of Obama's campaign advisors had spoken to Canadian officials to reassure them that Obama's anti-NAFTA talk "should be viewed as more about political positioning than a clear articulation of policy plans."[46]

Candidate Obama had to do some fancy campaign footwork to reassure his protectionist base that he opposed NAFTA. But nearly

---

44   United States. U.S. Chamber of Commerce. *Opening Markets, Creating Jobs: Estimated U.S. Employment Effects of Trade with FTA Partners.* 2010.

45   United States. U.S. Chamber of Commerce. *Trade Action—or Inaction: The Cost for American Workers and Companies.* September 15, 2009.

46   Palmer, Doug. "G20 Summit Could Give Doha Talks a Lift: WTO's Lamy." *ABC News.* September 22, 2010.

three years later, the Obama Administration hasn't touched NAFTA. So perhaps the campaign advisor's uncouth comment to the Canadians had been correct after all. Regardless, it's no secret why the Obama Administration has no interest in "renegotiating" NAFTA, or any such other nonsense:

- ▶ U.S. goods and services trade with Canada and Mexico totaled $1.1 trillion in 2008.
- ▶ Exports totaled $482 billion; imports totaled $596 billion.
- ▶ U.S. exports to Canada and Mexico in 2009 were $333.7 billion, up 135 percent from 1993 (the year prior to NAFTA).

It seems that President Obama has learned a thing or two since he was candidate Obama. Taking cheap shots at one of the greatest trade agreements in the nation's history is easy on the campaign trail and helps please the base, but when confronted with the undeniable benefits of the agreement, it's a little harder to keep campaign promises.

The president should be commended for his forceful defense of free trade in general. But the differences between candidate Obama and President Obama underscore the political challenge of championing free trade in the United States, especially for Democrats, but also for Republicans as well.

The opposition to free trade is easy enough to understand. Opponents say free trade undermines American manufacturing with an influx of cheap, foreign goods; free trade exploits workers in other countries that don't have labor laws or a minimum wage; and free trade ships jobs overseas, leaving hard-working Americans unemployed.

Certainly at a time of high U.S. unemployment, these arguments are compelling and attractive to many Americans, particularly union workers. With so many American industries, such as the steel and automotive industries, in various stages of collapse, Americans wonder if we can survive with a declining factory base. Indeed, the popular appeal of these arguments has led to government subsidies for manufacturers, to steel tariffs, and to multi-billion-dollar bail-outs of Detroit auto companies.

But the central fallacy of these arguments is that they see international trade as a zero-sum game. In other words, one nation must win, and one nation must lose. If a company shifts an American job overseas, that's one less job in America.

The reality is something different. Certain countries are better suited at producing certain products than other countries. Each country's economic prosperity will be much greater if it devotes its scarce resources to producing the products it is better suited and more efficient at producing, and then trading for those products it is less suited to produce.

So the reason that many factory jobs are leaving the United States is that generally other nations are more efficient at producing the same product. We might try to keep these jobs in the United States through artificial means, but since manufacturing in the United States is more costly, the overall economy suffers. It makes more sense for the United States to produce those products it is best suited to produce.

But making all products in the United States does not make sense. The beauty of free trade is that each country will do what it does best and that each company will make its own decision on where to manufacture, based on comparing costs and benefits. Every American executive would rather produce in the United States just as a matter of convenience. But when it's more efficient to produce the same product overseas and stay competitive within the industry, that executive will make a decision based on what's in the best interest of his or her company.

This comparison also holds true for the American workforce,

which is by far more educated than the workforces in high manufacturing countries, like China. Better educated people are more expensive to employ; better educated people also do not seek out factory jobs. Indeed, it is increasingly difficult to manufacture in the United States, not only for reasons of cost but also for finding workers who will be satisfied with factory jobs. People with college degrees do not want repetitive factory work.

As it is, we often face challenges filling the tens of millions of service jobs needed to keep our economy going. We cannot fill retail, fast food, cleaning, janitorial, gardening, driving, dishwashing, orderly, and other important and necessary jobs that are the backbone of our economy. One reason illegal immigrants are attracted to the United States is that many of these jobs are not filled, because Americans do not want them.

The kind of factory jobs Americans are filling are in the high-tech sectors, where educated workers are required to operate computers or work with complicated machinery. Instead of highly skilled Americans working in textile, steel, or automotive plants, they're working in computing, pharmaceutical, and nanotechnology plants.

BUY AMERICAN

The result of this shift away from more traditional factory jobs toward high-tech factory jobs is that the U.S. economy is more efficient and our workers are more productive. Our economy is able to generate more goods and consume more goods and services at a cheaper cost. We're doing what we do best, while other nations do what they do best. In the end, both win. International trade is not a zero-sum game.

Unfortunately, politics usually gets in the way. For instance, appeals like "Buy American" strike a patriotic chord, and on the surface it seems like the decent thing to do to help U.S. workers. But there's a wide chasm between the perception of "Buy American" and the reality.

In the 2009 "Recovery Act," which totaled $787 billion, there was a "Buy American" provision. All steel, iron, and manufactured products used in stimulus-funded projects had to be produced in the United States. The same was true for all clothing, equipment, and textile products used by the Department of Homeland Security. The obvious intent behind the "Buy American" provision was to create or save American jobs in these industries.

The problem occurs when other countries retaliate with "buy local" provisions of their own. For instance, the U.S Chamber of Commerce estimates:

> [a]ny net increases in U.S. employment resulting from the new "Buy American" provisions will quickly evaporate as other countries implement "buy national" policies of their own. In the event that retaliation causes U.S. companies to lose just 1 percent of potential foreign stimulus procurement opportunities, the net employment loss to the United States from the Recovery Act's "Buy American" provisions could total 176,800. In the event retaliation escalates, U.S. job losses will mount dramatically.[47]

Which raises the other ugly side of protectionist policies: whatever the United States can do to shut out foreign markets and goods, so those foreign countries can do to the United States. It happens all the time. Early in his term, for instance, President George W. Bush imposed steel tariffs on foreign producers as a boon to the domestic steel companies. At the time, the administration defended the move as a way to support an all-American industry. The cynics in the

---

47   United States. U.S. Chamber of Commerce. *Trade Action—or Inaction: The Cost for American Workers and Companies.* September 15, 2009.

audience saw it as an economically stupid way to buy votes in swing states like West Virginia and Pennsylvania.

In any case, three years after the imposition of the tariffs, the economic consequences proved too much. One study found that retaliation from foreign steel-producing countries had cost about 200,000 American manufacturing jobs, while steel prices rose as high as 30 percent, decimating the small steel-using shops across the country.[48] The administration finally waved the white flag and removed the tariffs.

Such economically short-sighted and politically motivated policies are one factor hindering the nation's economic growth. It happened under a Republican administration, and it's happening under a Democratic administration. Despite President Obama's best efforts, the main reason why nothing has been done to pass the pending free-trade agreements is because Democrats in Congress are beholden to the labor unions. Considering how much money the unions give to the Democratic Party, it's hard to blame them.

Since 1990, labor unions have contributed over $700 million (92 percent of union money) to Democrats. In 2008, unions contributed $68.2 million directly to the Democratic Party, according to the Center for Responsive Politics.[49] In addition, unions spent heavily on their own advertisements to get President Obama and other Democrats elected. The AFL-CIO borrowed over $30 million to support Democrats in the 2008 cycle. SEIU headquarters required every local affiliate to pay a $6 per member per month contribution or pay a 50 percent fine. The support of the Democrats does not come without strings. The unions expect something in return for their generous support of the Democratic Party, and

---

48 Allen, Mike and Jonathan Weisman. "Steel Tariffs Appeared to Have Backfired on Bush: 'Move to Aid Mills and Gain Votes in 2 States Is Called Political and Economic Mistake.'" *Washington Post*. September 19, 2003.

49 "Labor: Long-Term Contribution Trends." *Opensecrets.org*. October 25, 2010.

stalling passage of free-trade agreements is exactly what the unions had in mind.

It's not that Republicans are immune to patriotic appeals to "Buy American," but at least in the case of the GOP, we can assign it to pure economic ignorance. For Democrats, it's a shameful lesson in "pay-to-play" politics.

PIRACY

In terms of innovation, there remains the matter of intellectual property rights when it comes to free trade. The fact is that there is very little the United States can do to combat content piracy and patent stealing in foreign countries. Going abroad, it's easy to find a copy of almost any American movie or song at rock-bottom prices right off the street. World Trade Organization members are required to adhere to IP protections, but even these provisions are hard to enforce and violations hard to prove, except on a massive scale.

And the piracy isn't just movies and songs illegally downloaded over the Internet or burned onto a DVD. Sometimes foreign IP piracy takes the form of stolen computer codes and counterfeit consumer electronics. Most of these rip-offs are sold abroad, but they are also sometimes smuggled back into the United States and sold on the black market. This type of international IP piracy poses serious problems for innovative companies. Two recent examples highlight the severity of the problem.

> ▶ On June 8, 2010, a former research chemist for DuPont who had accepted a position at Peking University College of Engineering in China pleaded guilty to trade secret theft. In 2009, while still working for DuPont, he had attempted to

send documents detailing a proprietary chemical process and samples of chemical compounds to himself at the University.

► In July 2010, a former General Motors (GM) employee and her husband were arrested for selling GM trade secrets relating to hybrid-vehicle technology to Chery Automobile, a Chinese automotive manufacturer and a competitor of GM. GM estimated the value of the trade secrets to be more than $40 million.

Protecting our innovators' intellectual property, along with protecting American-style fair use rights, should be part of our free-trade policies. It doesn't help Apple to sell iPods to Colombia if some enterprising Colombian counterfeiter is going to take that iPod and produce it on the black market.

Here are some specific policy prescriptions:

Pass free-trade agreements with Panama, Colombia, and South Korea. These FTAs have been stalled in Congress for four years. Former Colombian President Alvaro Uribe said his one goal before leaving office in the summer of 2010 was to see the FTA with the United States ratified. It did not happen. In addition to the economic benefits, FTA agreements bring nations closer together. Colombia and Panama are honorable U.S. allies in an increasingly volatile region of the world. To keep their populations from embracing Hugo Chavez–style thuggery, we should be doing all we can to help grow their economy. Our message to them should be: there are benefits to allying yourself with the United States.

Encourage and enter worldwide trade negotiations and agreements. We should be seeking other free-trade opportunities worldwide. The United States should make reopening the

Doha Round a priority. Additionally, we need to keep the pressure on emerging nations like China, India, and Brazil to embrace international trade and to open their markets. Doha's success depends largely on these nations' willingness to play ball. As U.S. Trade Representative Ron Kirk said last year, "In order for the Doha Round to move forward, the world's big emerging economies must make their just contributions."[50]

Eliminate "Buy America" provisions from proposals and laws. Despite their patriotic intent, "Buy American" provisions end up hurting the American workforce. Forcing companies to do business with only American companies drives up costs on everyone. Moreover, foreign nations tend to retaliate with their own "buy local" provisions, leading to a vicious cycle of protectionist policies. Although we should always support and promote American industries, "Buy American" is a counterproductive way to do it.

Encourage foreign investors and businesses to do business here. Much like "Buy American" provisions, politicians are adept at criticizing foreign investment in the United States on patriotic grounds. For instance, in 2006, controversy swirled around a United Arab Emirates company's attempt to run six U.S. ports, because of national security fears. The critics' logic amounted to nothing more than that the UAE was in the Middle East and that there are terrorists in the Middle East, ergo, handing over management of U.S. ports was akin to inviting terrorists inside the country. It was pure demagoguery. The six ports were already owned by a British company. In any case, following the uproar, the deal eventually fell through.

---

50   Palmer, Doug. "G20 Summit Could Give Doha Talks a Lift: WTO's Lamy." *ABC.* September 22, 2010.

The United States needs foreign investment because it lowers the cost of capital for U.S. corporations. Moreover, we need foreign buyers to be able to come to the United States to purchase our goods. As the producer of the nation's largest trade show, the International CES, we see how our own government policies make it so difficult to host important buyers and officials from around the world. Every discouraged foreign buyer means a lost sale to a competitive country, or it means that American businesses have to travel overseas to try to make a sale.

Encourage and enforce clear and strong intellectual property policies. Our innovation and creativity in the United States and worldwide must be protected by strong intellectual property laws. However, these should focus on commercial piracy and be clear enough to allow innocent infringement and not dissuade innovation. Copyright laws can go too far. Innovation in America faces increasing hurdles from copyright laws that impose huge fines based on unclear definitions of when the law is violated. This chills innovation.

Trade with other nations is an emotional subject. Those who want us to close our borders and create new factories producing what we consume are well-meaning, but such protectionism would result in a Cuba-style economy.

There is no going back. Americans will prosper by being the most innovative country, and innovation requires access to all the world has to offer. America's innovators need free trade to innovate. If American politicians shut our doors while the world embraces free trade, we are on a path toward poverty.

8

Innovation Requires Good Schools

"Our nation is at risk. The educational foundations of our society are presently being eroded by a rising tide of mediocrity. If an unfriendly foreign power had attempted to impose on America the mediocre educational performance that exists today, we might well have viewed it as an act of war. We have, in effect, been committing an act of unthinking, unilateral educational disarmament. History is not kind to idlers."

—1983 report from the National Commission on Excellence in Education

LAGGING BEHIND

During President Reagan's first term, a blue-ribbon panel of prominent American government and private-sector appointees delivered a scathing evaluation of the nation's education system. The panel's final report, *A Nation at Risk: The Imperative for Educational Reform*, documented the declining performance of America's schools and proposed thirty-eight specific recommendations to meet the challenges.

The report dominated news cycles (back when those lasted longer than twenty minutes) for days, but the net result was . . . not much. On the report's twenty-fifth anniversary, an education advocacy group reported that "stunningly few" of the report's recommendations were ever enacted.[51]

We should have gotten a national wake-up call. Instead we hit the snooze button.

Since 1983, study after study has found U.S. students lagging behind their foreign counterparts across a broad range of subjects. Among the best-known studies is PISA, the Program for International Student Assessment, which measures the reading, math, and science literacy skills of fifteen-year-olds in OECD countries every three years.

In 2003, PISA found U.S. students were ahead of only five developed countries in terms of math skills. Students in thirty-one countries had higher average math literacy scores, including eight of the developing countries who also participated in the test. The 2006 PISA test found very similar results in science, with U.S. students in the bottom third of developed countries.[52] Six developing nations reported higher average scores than in the United States.

The same or similar results have been replicated across a wide variety of studies. And we can't explain away the findings by saying our best students are still fine. In math and science, "even the highest U.S. achievers . . . were outperformed on average by their OECD counterparts."

On the science test, twelve countries had students at the 90th percentile with higher scores than the United States. Math performance was even worse. U.S. students at the 90th percentile scored well below the OECD average on math literacy. Fully twenty-nine countries had higher scores at that level.

We are doing better in reading. The PISA 2000 test found that

---

51   United States. U.S. Department of Education. "A Nation at Risk." April 1983.

52   United States. U.S. Department of Education. Highlights From PISA 2006: Performance of U.S. 15-Year-Old Students in Science and Mathematics Literacy in an International Context. December 2007.

the performance of U.S. students was average overall but that the United States had a greater percentage of students performing at the highest level in reading.

The problem we now face is that innovation isn't something you can bottle and hand over to the next generation. We can't hoard it or ration it to keep progress going at a steady rate. It's a renewable resource, but it can only be cultivated indirectly.

An innovation economy can be damaged any number of ways, with bad government policies being right at the top of the list, but ground-breaking inventions have come from places ruled by even the most backward and benighted despots.

The one thing innovation truly needs to survive is an education system that adequately prepares the next generation of innovators. That's the raw material. That's why so many high-tech companies want to loosen visa limits to bring more highly educated scientists and engineers into the United States. They can't find enough here. This is why the decline of the American education system is a national tragedy. Reversing that decline must be a top national priority.

REALISM, NOT IDEOLOGY

When it comes to education reform, I'm a pragmatist. You don't have to have studied the education system for years to know we need good teachers working in superior educational environments backed by administrators with knowledge of local conditions and the power to manage according to results. This isn't that complicated.

Too many education debates get bogged down in large, systemic questions. Consider charter schools, which purport to offer a superior educational experience in exchange for more flexibility in how they run their operations. Millions of research dollars have been spent trying to answer the question of whether charter schools, as a concept, work. As the popular 2010 movie *Waiting for Superman* shows, some charter schools work much better than many urban schools.

The results have been contradictory so far, which isn't surprising. There are thousands of charter schools operating in the United States. Some of those schools are going to be great. Others won't be. What we should be spending our time on is figuring out why the good schools are so good, no matter how they are structured.

Unfortunately, the biggest problem with our education system is that it is dominated by entrenched interest groups that measure success less by student achievement and more by the economic welfare of their members. I'm talking, of course, about the teachers unions.

Understand that I'm not remotely anti-teacher. My father was a sixth-grade teacher, and my mother taught languages on the side. I can remember all the teachers I had in school who opened my eyes to the greater world and made learning the enjoyable activity it should be. Good teachers are one of the most precious resources we have.

The unions that represent them, however, are another story. And I say that despite the fact that my father was an active teachers union organizer and representative until he died in 2007.

For years, the National Education Association—which has an annual budget in excess of $300 million and more than 550 people on staff—has resisted every attempt to focus on teacher quality. The American Federation of Teachers has marched in lock-step behind them. As a result of their efforts, it can be practically impossible to fire an underperforming teacher without endless delays or crippling legal challenges.

For a look at how bad teachers can linger forever, you can't do better than the award-winning *New Yorker* article by Steven Brill, "The Rubber Room," detailing the way New York City spent hundreds of millions of dollars annually to warehouse hundreds of alcoholic, abusive, inept, lazy, incompetent, or misaligned teachers.[53]

The problem is the state's tenure system, which guarantees nearly every teacher a job for life once they complete three years in the classroom. It takes years of long, drawn-out hearings and appeals to force out even the most incompetent teachers; at the time of the *New Yorker* story, warehoused teachers had been out of the classroom an average of three years, with full pay and benefits during that entire time—*and many still weren't close to a resolution of their cases.*

As one principal explained the situation, the union "would protect a dead body in the classroom." And even a 2009 partial New York City compromise with the union allowing rubber room teachers to be assigned work was challenged in 2010 because teachers complained the work might be outside the area of the rubber room.

Getting bad teachers out of the classroom—and good teachers in— is a critically important component of any reform effort. A 2007 study funded by the non-partisan Brookings Institute found that a student with a first-rate teacher could expect a ten-point jump in standardized test performance after just one year. The study's authors note:

[T]he black-white achievement gap nationally is roughly 34 percentage points. Therefore, if the effects were to accumulate, having a top-quartile teacher rather than a bottom-quartile teacher four years in a row would be enough to close the black–white test score gap.[54]

These results are astounding, and they support what everyone knows—good teachers matter.

Even in the face of such evidence, the teachers unions reject completely the idea of pay for performance. They seem to think edu-

---

53   Brill, Steven. "The Rubber Room." *The New Yorker.* Aug. 31, 2009.

54   Bendor, Joshua, et al. "An Education Strategy to Promote Opportunity, Prosperity, and Growth." The Brookings Institution. February 2007.

cation is the one industry in America where we aren't allowed to acknowledge that there are higher and lower performers, and pay people accordingly.

In Washington, D.C., where forward-thinking school superintendent Michelle Rhee actually fired several hundred teachers in 2009 and 2010, the union retaliated. It contributed over $1 million to defeat the mayor—so that Michelle Rhee would go away. The union succeeded.

There is hope. The *Los Angeles Times* (under the leadership of its president, Eddie Hartenstein) actually published the results of each Los Angeles teacher's performance in raising average test scores. Brilliant! Why teachers unions defend the worst teachers is unclear. It hurts good teachers, and it hurts students.

Teachers want to teach. That's why they became teachers. But we would do a better job retaining the very best teachers if we could reward them for their dedication—and results—in the classroom.

Of course, pay for performance already happens. Because education is funded primarily by local property taxes, schools in more affluent areas can afford to pay higher salaries. The best teachers in adjoining districts are often recruited into the higher-paying system.

But rather than support plans that might keep more of those qualified teachers working in underprivileged systems, the unions have fought to keep their guaranteed, across-the-board salary increases based almost solely on seniority. It's time for Americans to say "enough" and insist that differential pay for teachers be instituted based on teacher competence, subject matter, and skills.

SUBJECT MATTERS

Subject matter, well, *matters* because, as discussed above, we need to focus on math and science education as a nation. Lack of emphasis on science and math was the biggest issue with the No Child Left Behind Act. This legislation had any number of benefits, but it also had the unintended consequence of putting an intense focus on basic English and math at the cost of de-emphasizing science education.

We do need to teach the basics—good old reading, writing, and arithmetic—but those are mere stepping stones to greater knowledge. We need intense science education not just to train the next generation of scientists and engineers but also because so many of the global problems we face require elementary science knowledge to understand. Think how much more informed important debates like climate change (and frivolous debates like evolution) would be if all Americans were truly comfortable with the scientific method.

We also must teach history, civics, and economics. The founders understood that an informed citizenry was a requirement for democracy to flourish. Our students must understand the true nature of America, its past, and the greatness it has inspired throughout history.

9

Innovation Requires Competitive Broadband

"I arrived at the web because the 'Enquire' (E not I) program—short for Enquire Within Upon Everything, named after a Victorian book of that name full of all sorts of useful advice about anything—was something I found really useful for keeping track of all the random associations one comes across in Real Life and brains are supposed to be so good at remembering but sometimes mine wouldn't. It was very simple but could track those associations which would sometimes develop into structure as ideas became connected, and different projects become involved with each other."

—TIM BERNERS-LEE, 1995[55]

WHY WE NEED BROADBAND

You just read how one man created the World Wide Web. He, along with Dr. Robert Kahn and Vint Cerf, are the undisputed fathers of the Internet. (Former Congressman Rick Boucher actually helped birth the Internet by pushing policies allowing its commercial life.) But Berners–Lee's description of the idea isn't very interesting, is it?

---

55   Berners–Lee, Tim. "Frequently Asked Questions." *W3.org.*

In fact, were I a venture capitalist and a potential investment walked in my office spouting that jargon, I'd quickly show him the door. Little would I know that I'd just kicked out a guy whose idea helped generate $3.7 trillion in sales in the United States in 2009 alone. I guess that's why I still have a day job.

Two things happened in 1989 that would forever change the way we live, work, play, and learn. The first was English computer scientist Tim Berners-Lee's proposal of "hypertext" as a way to share information among researchers worldwide. The idea led directly to the creation of the World Wide Web. The second was the official launch of America Online, which at its peak would be the online gateway for more than 30 million U.S. subscribers.

These two ideas did more than anything to change the Internet from an academic and research tool into the single biggest driver of innovation in the past two decades. In the twenty-first century, broadband Internet has become the indispensable utility. It connects, educates, equalizes, and uplifts all who receive it.

Which is why it's so disappointing that the United States continues to fall behind other countries on virtually every important measure of broadband availability and quality. It didn't have to be that way. Fortunately, we have a new opportunity to leap back to the front, if only we can muster the political will to overcome entrenched interests and make it happen.

Let's go back to another important year in the history of the Internet. In 1996, Congress recognized the tectonic changes taking place in the telecommunications industry and passed a law intended to break up the old local phone monopolies and finally promote real competition and innovation.

The law is almost as notable for what it doesn't contain as for what it does. As enacted by Congress, the complete text of the act runs 128 pages. You'll find "Internet" in there, but the words "Web" and "e-mail" don't appear a single time. "Broadband" shows up just once. And you can spend all night looking, but you won't find "Skype," "Wikipedia," or "YouTube."

Congress can hardly be faulted for failing to include things that hadn't been invented yet, but the pace of technological change since 1996 has been both dizzying and exhilarating. Affordable broadband Internet technology actually predates both the Web and the America Online dial-up service, ironically enough. Researchers in Bell Labs first invented the technology that would become DSL in the 1980s. Unfortunately, the Bell-era monopoly phone companies had little incentive to market a product that would cut into their highly profitable businesses selling more expensive alternatives like T1s and second phone lines. So the technology sat on the shelf for years. Only after Congress opened up the industry could new competitors finally jump into the market with their own DSL services, while cable providers began their own broadband revolution by unleashing cable modem service.

For a brief moment, it looked like the century-old monopolies might finally fade away and competition would fully replace regulation as the engine behind broadband deployment. Consumers began to gain a real choice among broadband providers, and new alternatives were being launched seemingly every week. All that competition was spurring innovation and driving down prices, as it always does.

Unfortunately for most of us here in the United States, those exciting times have not yet created a robustly competitive broadband marketplace for all Americans. While other countries have continued implementing policies designed to make broadband faster and more affordable, regulators in the United States have been hesitant to fully embrace competition as the most effective tool in promoting broadband deployment. A sputtering regulatory regime, subject to abrupt reversals of policy as administrations have changed, has handicapped new entrants and left many markets dominated by a monopoly or a duopoly in broadband service—hardly the ideal rec-ipe for innovation and progress. Although existing telephone and cable companies have been pioneers in broadband deployment and continue to make innovative new services available to consumers, more competitors would bring more innovation and more choice.

The results of our slow move toward broadband competition are stark. According to the OECD, the United States ranks fifteenth in terms of the percentage of households with broadband Internet access.[56] Our average connection speeds are just a half to a third of those of global leaders like Hong Kong and South Korea.[57] Barring a completely unforeseen shift in the national regulatory structure, wireline broadband competition is on hold. The future will have to be wireless.

Wireless broadband avoids many of the disadvantages intrinsic to traditional copper or fiber optic networks:

Cost. Laying cable is incredibly expensive. In comparison, a wireless network can go up anywhere you can find a tall building to bolt your equipment onto.

Scalability. Wireless services can be built to meet real-time demand. As traffic increases, providers can just add an antenna. (Although, as we'll see, there are some limitations we're now facing.)

Portability. There's a reason so many homes have Wi-Fi networks: No one wants to be chained to one place for accessing the Internet.

---

56   Organisation For Economic Co-Operation And Development. "OECD Broadband Portal." June 10, 2010.

57   Belson, David. "State of the Internet 2010. 2nd Quarter. 2010 Report." *Akamai.* Vol. 1 No. 2.

Disaster recovery. In the event of a natural or "man-caused" disaster, it can take weeks to repair cut or downed lines. Wireless services work as soon as power can be restored at both ends of the connection.

SPECTRUM PROBLEMS

There is a problem, though, which is that the spectrum currently allocated for wireless communications services in the United States is getting awfully crowded. Indeed, as iPhone users in many cities know firsthand, companies are facing challenges accommodating the huge growth in wireless broadband demand. As the United States leads the world in creativity and applications ("apps"), this looming spectrum crisis needs to be addressed.

As with many of our nation's problems, the answer is obvious and not that complicated, but standing in the way is a powerful interest group. In this case, it's the television broadcaster's lobby.

I won't deny the nation's broadcasters are in a quandary. Their business model relies on the incredibly inefficient use of hundreds of billions of dollars worth of high-quality wireless spectrum that was loaned to them for free by the American people.

At the same time, their market share has dropped from 100 percent, when the government first gave them that valuable property more than seventy-five years ago, to less than 10 percent today. In a world with cable, satellite, and Internet TV alternatives, there's little need for a redundant over-the-air broadcast system. (For those television viewers who cannot afford pay service, numerous studies have shown that subsidizing their connection to a "pay" service can be done for a tiny fraction of the money that the reclaimed spectrum would bring at auction.)

Unfortunately, confronted with the inarguable fact that our nation is running out of wireless spectrum, and that broadband is a bipartisan national priority, broadcasters have repeatedly worked to block proposals to reallocate the nation's spectrum more efficiently.

Let's look at the facts. Wireless broadband networks are reaching a choke point. The FCC reports that we need at least 500 megahertz of spectrum just to keep up with demand for broadband service. The nation's broadcasters use only a portion of the hundreds of megahertz of high-quality spectrum that we let them use for free. Reallocating some of that spectrum for broadband services would allow over-the-air televison to continue while still solving our wireless crisis.

We are truly in deep trouble as a nation if we can't reallocate a public resource that leaders across the political spectrum agree we desperately need to use in a different way if we're going to stay globally competitive. This is especially true when the business squatting on this spectrum borrowed it without paying taxpayers and when the terms of the loan indicate that it is for a limited period of time and subject to the "public interest."

It's time to require broadcasters to return at least half their present spectrum by 2015. Given the political strength of broadcasters, it seems that government cannot simply reclaim the spectrum it lent them, so broadcasters may have to be paid out of the proceeds of repurposing this spectrum for better use. It's an unfortunate reality, but it's worth it to avoid years of costly litigation and ever more crammed wireless networks.

The high prices this spectrum is expected to attract would be an appropriate market-based incentive to ensure its future use. For broadcasters facing declining market share and revenues—a 26 percent drop since 2005, according to the FCC—voluntary spectrum auctions would provide a revenue windfall.

Most of this spectrum should be auctioned off for use as wireless broadband. We should expect significant interest to come from companies that haven't historically been in the Internet Service

Provider business, like perhaps Google (or the next Google). That's how much potential this spectrum has.

A portion of the spectrum should be allocated for unlicensed purposes. These frequencies—like the ones on which your cordless phone and garage door opener operate—would be open for any non-interfering use.

We should do this because the reclaimed television spectrum is so valuable that only deep-pocketed companies will be able to make the investments needed to win those auctions. But if there's one thing we know, it's that innovation often comes from start-ups— from someone who has an idea and sets out to design, build, and sell a product based on that idea.

Unlicensed spectrum will allow smaller players to play that innovative role and will ensure innovative new technologies aren't blocked from reaching the marketplace, the same way DSL once was.

The 1900s were the era of broadcasting, but now we are in the Internet century. We cannot let an old business model hog government property any more than we would have granted horse-and-buggy makers exclusive use of the public roads after the invention of the car.

Our nation needs broadband access for the thousands of new businesses and millions of jobs it will create, for the scientists and doctors it will educate, and for the connections to developing economies across the globe it will forge.

I have personally advocated for broadband since the mid 1990s. Back then, I spoke repeatedly about how generations often benefit from one innovative infrastructure technology that spurred investment and a shift upward in quality of life. Consider how plumbing, electricity, the telephone, and cable TV each changed the average American's life and even the home construction industry.

The difference with broadband is that one option per household isn't enough. You probably don't put much thought into your toilet.

It either works or it doesn't, and the rates you pay are well-regulated and nominal.

Internet access doesn't operate the same way. One size doesn't fit all. And as service providers continue pushing for the right to discriminate or charge more for certain types of Internet traffic, real concerns are starting to emerge.

The Net Neutrality issue is a good example of why government involvement should be limited to those areas where there are substantial market or regulatory failures.

Net Neutrality is the concept that a broadband service provider (like cable or a telephone company) should not be able to block out access to Web sites that it views as competitors. The cable and telephone companies correctly claim that the market is working and they have rarely blocked Web site access for competitive purposes. But Internet companies and other businesses that rely on the ability to be accessed by consumers with a click of a mouse are concerned and want the government to mandate Net Neutrality.

There is a middle-ground approach. Rather than attempting to develop ironclad rules for a rapidly shifting marketplace, we should institute a national policy favoring competition, combined with easy termination options, to allow consumers to choose what type of broadband service they want to purchase, without worrying that their two-year contract locks them into a service that blocks YouTube videos.

We should also encourage broadband deployment through incremental steps, such as allowing employers to pay for employee broadband at home as taxable benefit. This alone will encourage massive broadband deployment. It will also encourage telework, getting cars off our highways and helping us take the steps needed to address climate change. Another great idea pushed by Minnesota Senator Amy Klobuchar and California Representative Anna Eshoo is to require that underground broadband lines be laid for every federally supported transportation project.

The current FCC is to be applauded for its courage in adopting a National Broadband Plan that calls for the redeployment of desperately needed wireless spectrum for use in innovative new broadband services. Under chairman Julius Genachowski's leadership, the commission worked in a bipartisan manner to adopt a robust plan that, if implemented, would protect our nation from the looming spectrum crisis that threatens our world dominance in broadband. The National Broadband Plan is bold—it challenges incumbent industries while embracing next generation technology and innovation as engines of economic recovery and growth. While the plan requires Congress to take additional steps to implement, it has the support of the president and of many in Congress as well as the technology sector and consumer groups. It is my fervent hope that entrenched incumbent industries that refuse to innovate will be unsuccessful in their effort to block progress on this plan.

For far too long, the United States—the birthplace of the Internet—has lagged behind other developed companies in terms of broadband penetration and innovation. It's time for that to change.

10

Government Spending: Imperiling Innovation and More

"The budget should be balanced, the Treasury should be refilled, public debt should be reduced, the arrogance of officialdom should be tempered and controlled, and the assistance to foreign lands should be curtailed lest Rome become bankrupt. People must again learn to work, instead of living on public assistance."

—CICERO, 55 BC

REAL GROWTH VERSUS GOVERNMENT SPENDING

As a matter of fact, Cicero never said this. As discovered by Paul Boller and John George in their book, *They Never Said It: A Book of Fake Quotes, Misquotes, and Misleading Attributions*, the quote, which has been widely circulated, was a 1986 newspaper fabrication. Nevertheless, I couldn't find a better quote, so, with apologies to Marcus Tullius Cicero, I'm sticking with it because it perfectly captures the importance of good governance.

Our tale of two cities is the story of how Washington, D.C., like Cicero's Rome, has grown out of control at the direct expense of our once-thriving private sector, with Detroit as one very painful example. As a nation, we have largely forgotten that every single dollar of government spending is either paid by present taxpayers or borrowed from future taxpayers. In other words, there is no such thing as a free lunch from our government. Unless we return to governing on the basis of this truth, our economy and entire nation are at grave risk.

Earlier, we examined why innovation is the key to real growth in our economy and jobs. But innovation in the U.S. is being strangled by national policies that threaten to condemn future generations to stagnation and decline, and it all starts with massive government spending.

U.S. government spending is entirely divorced from any economic reality. In 2009, our federal government spent $3.5 trillion. This compares to $2.5 trillion spent in 2005, a 40 percent increase in only four years. Moreover, in 2009 the feds collected $2.1 trillion in taxes and fees, resulting in an annual deficit of $1.4 trillion. And according to the *most* optimistic Obama Administration forecast of future deficits, the total debt will grow to a minimum of $11 trillion in 2019. This level of debt would be 82 percent of our GDP, double the level of 41 percent in 2008.

But our national situation is much, much worse than that. Add in $2.5 trillion in state and local debt, $3 trillion in unfunded state pension liabilities, *$106 trillion* in unfunded Social Security and Medicare liabilities, and $1 trillion in unfunded state health care and other benefits, and a more realistic projection of future federal deficits (in light of such initiatives as Obamacare and total U.S. debt obligations) amount to "$130 trillion or so, or just under ten times the official national debt" according to one estimate.[58]

Much has been written about the financial problems of Social Security and Medicare, so I won't rehash those matters. However, it's only recently that the financial time-bomb of public unions

---

58   Williamson, Kevin. "The Other National Debt." *National Review Online.* June 14, 2010.

has been recognized, so a few words about that are appropriate. I'll begin by betting that you don't know that the U.S. Bureau of Labor Statistics reports that, in 2009, the number of government union workers (7.9 million) for the first time in our history exceeded the number of private sector union workers (7.4 million). And given the further expansion of government and the contraction of the private sector since 2009, this differential has undoubtedly grown.

As noted above, the public union problem is primarily one of unfunded pension and health-care liabilities. The federal government and nearly every state and local government have committed to defined benefit plans for their full-time employees. These programs are massive: the federal retirement program supports more than 2.5 million annuitants. The fifty states and thousands of local governments support more than 8 million annuitants. The payouts are generous because most payouts are based on years of service and total compensation in the worker's final year. For example, the annual payout to retirees generally is 2–3 percent per year of service multiplied by final compensation. Thus, a fifty-two-year-old worker making $100,000 in his final year before retiring could get $90,000 per year for life, not counting lifetime medical benefits.

Predictably, our federal government is already shifting funds to state and local governments to help pay for their plans. About one-third of 2009's nearly $800 billion "stimulus" package and the entire summer 2010 sweetener stimulus went to states, primarily to enable state government to both avoid layoffs and pay pension obligations. No one knows what will happen when the stimulus plan funds to states run out in 2011.

The massive federal debt destroys future private sector investment because the only ways to pay off this staggering level of debt are to (a) increase taxes and (b) print more money, which will drastically lower the future value of the dollar. Both actions lower the returns that private sector investors can earn. Moreover, the riskier an investment, the greater the return that investors need to compensate for the risk, and innovation investments are invariably among the most risky, so they will be disproportionately ravaged, crushing economic growth and job creation.

UNCERTAINTY

But the devastating results for innovation from such massive government spending go beyond higher taxes and a debased dollar. First, out-of-control debt directly increases overall economic uncertainty among private sector investors, significantly complicating their investment decision-making and further reducing investment. Second, as we are seeing in the present economic crisis, our government typically responds to economic turmoil by significantly increasing and expanding regulation of business, which increases costs, lowers investment returns, and further increases uncertainty.

In fact, a September 2010 report issued by the SBA Office of Advocacy found that rules and restrictions imposed by the federal government now cost Americans some $1.75 trillion annually, up 60 percent in less than five years. The report also says that the cost per employee of these regulations is higher for small firms than for large firms. And a recent conference on the 2002 Sarbanes-Oxley Act held by the American Enterprise Institute found that:

> . . . the process of nurturing innovative and high-tech start-up companies has been slowed [because] the high cost of becoming and remaining a public company has made an initial public offering (IPO) financially impractical for many small companies, which

in turn has narrowed the options of the venture capital firms that have usually provided seed money financing for risky high-tech start-ups.[59]

Uncertainty causes all private investment to wither, and innovation investments wither the most. For example, venture capital (VC) firms, which have financed such successful start-ups as Intel, Microsoft, Google, and eBay, typically have an investment horizon of five to seven years. Unless VCs have reasonable certainty about tax and regulatory policies over this horizon, their risks will skyrocket, and their innovation investments will shrink.

As a final note about our desperate financial situation, consider that as annual deficits build up our mountain of debt, the annual interest on that debt will account for an ever greater share of annual spending, leaving less for good and essential programs. Interest payments are expected soon to reach more than $500 billion, exceeding the entire annual defense budget, leading U.S. military commanders to warn Congress that this is a grave threat to our nation. The 2009 "stimulus" alone added $280 a month to the debt of every American citizen. Put another way, the 2009 $1.4 trillion deficit means that future generations will have to pay $58 billion annually just to serve the single year 2009 deficit (assuming a 5 percent interest rate and no principal payments). The 2009 total U.S. accumulated debt of $7 trillion requires $350 billion in annual interest payments using this formula.

To put the interest issue in non-technical terms, consider this recent observation by columnist George Will:

In 1916, in Woodrow Wilson's first term, the richest man in America, John D. Rockefeller, could have written a personal check and

---

59   "Are Regulatory Costs Impeding Innovation?" *American Enterprise Institute*. May 10, 2007.

retired the national debt. Today, the richest man in America, Bill Gates, could write a personal check for all his worth and not pay two months interest on the national debt. By 2015, debt service will consume about one-quarter of individual income taxes. Ten years from now the three main entitlements—Medicare, Medicaid, and Social Security—plus interest will consume 93 percent of all federal revenues. Twenty years from now debt service will be the largest item in the federal budget.[60]

SOLUTIONS

What can be done? Our federal government never reduces spending, seldom cuts obsolete or ineffective programs, increases the complexity of taxes (the Internal Revenue Code is at more than 3.4 million words and counting), and incessantly augments the scope of business regulation. And then our politicians appear dumbfounded that our economy is struggling and jobs are scarce.

I believe our situation is so dire that we cannot talk about merely slowing the rate of government spending. Instead, our goal must be to cut the spending, and cut it past the point where it symbolically "hurts." I liken this to the medical strategy in war and other major crises where the resources are limited compared to all possible needs: triage. This is where the injured are divided into three groups: those who can survive without immediate medical attention, those who need immediate medical attention to survive, and those who are almost certain to die and will receive no attention other than painkillers.

Similarly, our government needs to triage its spending to those programs most important to our future, especially the future of

---

60   Will, George. "Not a State-Broken People." *Real Clear Politics*. July 26, 2010.

our children. In doing so, we will stop spending for programs and people that either do not need or do not deserve taxpayer funding, focusing instead on those programs and people that need and deserve taxpayer funding.

If you doubt my sincerity about this approach, consider my opinions and behavior when confronted with government spending that would have benefitted the industry I am paid to represent. As indicated earlier, the Consumer Electronics Association has never asked the government to spend money to benefit our industry. This was awkward for me when I was testifying before Congress.

Democrat and Republican members pressed me to specify how they could get money to consumers to subsidize the transition from analog television to digital television. They were concerned that consumers, especially poor and elderly consumers who did not own digital TVs or get cable or satellite service, would lose television service when the analog service was cut off. I consistently responded with data challenging the extent of the problem. (Both the Congressional Research Service and the National Association of Broadcasters had data that indicated the "at risk" population was almost double the size we had estimated—but we at CEA were quickly proved to be correct). I told Congress then that we did not advocate that the government spend money on this program. Nevertheless, despite our lack of support, Congress allocated $1.2 billion to provide each American family two $40 coupons toward the purchase of an analog-to-digital converter box for use on analog televisions. This subsidy would go to members of the CEA who made these boxes— but I am proud the CEA was never on record as supporting it.

To some extent, the coupon program was the political price Americans had to pay for a transition that would bring in an estimated $20 billion in revenue for the U.S. Treasury (from auctioning off spectrum freed by the analog signal cut off). In any event, I then threw myself and CEA into working to make the transition succeed. I sought my counterparts from the cable and broadcasting industries, and the three of us quickly agreed to work together to inform the American public about the February 17, 2009 transition. We solicited some two hundred groups to support our efforts and, within months, had gone from near zero awareness of the transition to nearly 100 percent awareness among Americans of the February 17 transition date.

Along the way, in 2007, I was summoned to the office of the Federal Trade Commissioner (now Chairman), Jon Lebowitz. Commissioner Lebowitz expressed concern about public confusion about the transition and asked whether I thought the FTC should get involved to regulate how the message on the transition was conveyed. I said that he should keep this in perspective: a few people might lose television service for a few days. I suggested he compare this to the fact that millions of people were signing mortgage documents when they bought their homes which they simply did not understand, and this would likely result in them losing their homes. Hearing that, he agreed.

But true to form, the government managed to turn a straightforward program into another boondoggle paid for by our taxpayers. Only days away from the February 17 analog shut-off, the demand for coupons was strong, as we had projected. But the government bean counters had assumed that every request for a $40 coupon counted as a government expenditure. At the peak of program demand, they said they had run out of money, and they stopped sending coupons.

A simple fix would have been for Congress to allow them to use historical redemption rates and even provide a modest amount of back-up funding authority in case demand and redemptions exceeded projections. Indeed, this was the bipartisan approach being discussed. But some Obama advisers had convinced the president-elect that the transition date had to be delayed and that more funding had to be provided. So before he even was sworn in, Obama asked Congress for another $250 million in funding and to delay the transition date until June 12, 2009. We at the CEA opposed the delay and the entire financial request, even though it meant more money to our industry.

In the end, Congress decided to spend an additional billion dollars, which was a total waste of money. Just about everyone in Congress knew it was a waste, but being frugal in spending taxpayer funds was less important to the Democrats in the majority than not crossing the new President. If we had stuck with the February 17 date, at worse a few Americans would have lost television service for a few days. Despite representing television and converter box makers, I keep asking how losing television service for a few days compares to how that money could have been used for important things like cutting the deficit or educating our children.

LEADERSHIP MATTERS

Fortunately, we have some politicians who are also demonstrating common sense and backbone in response to our crises. Case in point is Minnesota governor Tim Pawlenty, a Republican who inherited a financially troubled state but turned the state's finances around simply through priority setting and discipline. In a column for Politico, he wrote:

> Not everything the government does is equally important. When faced with a budget shortfall in Minnesota, we considered the importance of programs. We decided to protect funding for the most important ones: the National Guard, veterans' support programs, public safety and K–12 schools. Nearly everything else has been cut. [In 2009] we cut overall spending for the first time in the state's 150 year history.[61]

---

61   Pawlenty, Tim. "Time for Obama to Make Sacrifices." *Politico.com*. July 14, 2010.

This is triage of government spending in action, as well as courageous political leadership in action. Along with Governor Chris Christie of New Jersey and a few other politicians, Governor Pawlenty is demonstrating what must be done and can be done to reverse our economic fortunes.

In the next chapter, I suggest some principles and strategies to help extract our country from our economic mess and once again put us on the path to real growth in our economy and jobs. But I should end this chapter with a paean to leaders like Governors Pawlenty and Christie.

Leadership matters because it sets a tone for governing and gives a behavior example for all of us. It matters both in the private sector and the public sector. It has been regularly and widely written about, but it's doubtful too much can be made of it. Fortunately, when real leadership is demonstrated, it galvanizes clear-minded citizens and rewards those leaders; and when it is absent, it is readily apparent, disappointing to those same citizens and unrewarding to those who fail the leadership test.

Americans see vivid examples of top government officials repeatedly failing to lead on matters of fiscal responsibility and integrity. They see it when the President travels to another city by Air Force One for a date to see a show and have a meal, and when the first lady takes her daughter to Europe for a vacation at a cost to U.S taxpayers approaching a million dollars. They see it when the Commerce Department takes out a $2 million, thirty-second ad on the Super Bowl to promote the Census. They see it when the Obama Administration insists on putting terrorists on trial in a major U.S. city and ignores the additional security costs of $150 to $200 million compared to a relatively inexpensive and secure trial in the demonized Guantanamo base. They see it in the lavish pensions and gifts Congressional leaders bestow on themselves when they retire.

I vividly remember a 2007 meeting in Washington with two top executives from Best Buy and Circuit City. The Circuit City executive had flown on the company's private jet from Richmond (barely 100 miles away) and had been picked up in a stretch limousine to be taken to our meeting. In contrast, the Best Buy executive flew the cheapest commercial flight possible from its Minneapolis headquarters—a dawn flight to Dulles Airport—despite the inconvenient time and location. He then took a bus to the Washington Metro, where he boarded the subway to our meeting place. At the time, Circuit City was in financial trouble whereas Best Buy was doing well, but the Best Buy's executive's message of frugality resonated positively through his company.

In the incredibly competitive, cost-conscious consumer electronics industry, this focus on spending prevails. Crutchfield, Wal-Mart, and Panasonic are somewhat famous for their focus on costs, and their leadership not only talks the frugal talk but walks the frugal walk.

Similarly, I was impressed when Britain's new leader, David Cameron, flew a commercial jet to the United States, explaining that he was cutting government spending and raising taxes and needed to lead by example.

Yes, leadership matters. And leadership with integrity matters even more.

11

Government Spending: Modest Proposals to Restore Sanity

INFRASTRUCTURE

The five-hour drive in a rickety old bus from New Delhi to the Taj Mahal is one I wish every American could take. It is not that the road is unpaved or bumpy; in fact most of the trip is on a straight road of smooth concrete. Nor is it the multitude of animals, over-loaded rickshaws, vehicles of every type going every speed, or the constant blaring of horns that stand out in my mind. The confusing cacophony and constant shifts in speed are at first amusing and then just accepted as part of the reality of Indian transportation.

Rather, it is the human misery. On my 2008 trip, this unbelievable impression I had as we drove is one that has stuck with me. I just kept thinking we were in the bad part of town and would soon be out of it. We never did get out of it. The abject poverty, the beggars, the high incidence of deformity, and the medley of people living alongside the garbage simply trying to survive under the deplorable conditions—which includes oppressive heat and undrinkable water, inadequate plumbing, and hardly any electricity—this is what has stayed with me. Meanwhile every American takes these basic services for granted.

Americans just assume the basics of life: shelter, clean water, electricity, safe food, and a functioning toilet. Few Americans give real thought to our bounty, our luck, and our health. All were the result of the huge sacrifice and investment our predecessors made so that we could live this comfortable life with heat in winter, air conditioning in summer, wonderful showers, clean parks, schools, libraries, highways, working plumbing, and clean air. The average American has over twenty-five consumer electronics products, and the electricity that makes them work is just simply assumed.

But our future is clouded by a lack of investment in the most basic infrastructure. Our bridges are crumbling; our water systems were designed to last only fifty years, and many are hitting their limit; and our politicians refuse to invest in infrastructure.

Moreover, our partisan political system makes infrastructure a low priority. Republicans use infrastructure debates to find deficit discipline. Combined with their refusal to raise taxes of any kind, Republicans often see infrastructure investment as a politically painless way to cut the deficit. On the other extreme, Democrats fight to make all government-funded infrastructure projects as expensive as possible. For Democrats, infrastructure projects are ways to boost employment numbers, which is why they insist that union labor be used for all these projects. So this unhealthy political elixir of financial prudence, tax-increase avoidance, and union protectionism combine to deny Americans real investment in infrastructure.

When the parties' political worlds suddenly combine to allow an investment in infrastructure, they do so in political rather than strategic fashion. Thus the 2009 stimulus packages were more a wish list of "shovel-ready" projects designed to gather votes and protect political constituencies, rather than focused attempts at rebuilding our crumbling systems. It was like hiring lots of painters to spruce up the house while ignoring the termites destroying the home's foundation.

President Reagan had the courage and leadership to propose and obtain a five cent per gallon of gasoline tax increase to fund infrastructure. This example is valid today, and these types of user taxes are necessary, for any entity, for long-term survival. So while activists and the *New York Times* editorial page harp on the "rights" of every group to use taxpayer money and government intervention to obtain equal status, I am more concerned that our entire nation is moving to second- or third-world status.

When our electricity flickers and shuts down more frequently, our running water becomes polluted, and our bridges and streets and highways crack and break, then we will blame our government. Only when we can't heat our homes will we ask the government to respond immediately to ease the crisis, when what we should be doing is accepting that tough decisions are necessary *now* to avoid the certainty of a collapse of a geriatric infrastructure. We are becoming India, and it saddens and angers me.

I mention this now in a chapter on ways to cut our suicidal deficit because I want to be clear about my position on government spending. Not all massive government projects are bad. But they need a focus, they need a strategy, they need to be started with the expectation that we are solving a grave national threat. Our crumbling infrastructure represents just such a threat. When Americans are worried that there's not going to be enough electricity to power their lights, they aren't going to be worried about innovating the next great product. Innovation is defined by the context in which it occurs. No one in the Middle Ages could have invented an iPod, even if Steve Jobs traveled back in time and gave someone every detail of the design. Similarly, no American will invent the next iPod or smartphone if we cannot provide clean water.

Infrastructure investment requires resource allocation. Briefly, some principles for infrastructure include:

- ► Any federal funding should be matched by state and local governments.
- ► Excise taxes can be used for funding as appropriate: gasoline taxes for highways, water taxes for water, etc.
- ► Projects should be selected outside the political realm by an independent commission. Decisions must be based on expert assessment using objective criteria (impact, age, etc.).
- ► Congress should be forced to vote up or down on the independent panel's recommendations. (This process has been successfully used to decide which military bases should close.)

Our politicians are getting in the way of ensuring that the quality of life all Americans take for granted will be there for the next generation.

CUTTING THE DEFICIT

What neither Republicans nor Democrats have the courage to tell the American people is that if we want to put the country on a sound fiscal path, it's going to take hard, painful choices. There is no other way. Some of the following proposals might seem harsh; others, I'll admit, are a bit peculiar. But it's the kind of unconventional thinking that we need our lawmakers to be engaged in, as opposed to the popular but insignificant call to "end earmarks."

The abomination of our federal government's annual spending is beyond the scope of this book to definitively address. Instead, I will set forth some highly personal opinions about the principles that should guide our citizens and our politicians. I'll start with some first principles.

The first role of federal government is to protect our nation. No challenge of government is greater than protecting its citizens, and in this global community that means national defense is the single most important priority for government programs and spending.

The second role of federal government is to protect our citizens domestically—through courts and a criminal justice system. This is obvious to most of us, but somehow we have created a legal system that appears to have morphed beyond reason so that politically motivated prosecutors can bring charges against anyone for violations as vague as "insider trading" or RICO (Racketeer Influenced and Corrupt Organization Act) charges. In 2010, the Supreme Court recognized this when it unanimously threw out financial charges based on "theft of service," a crucial underpinning of many RICO legal actions.

Our long-lasting war on drugs has been an expensive failure, costing taxpayers billions of dollars in judicial, penal, and incarceration programs. Struggling local police departments now pursue marijuana violators because they receive federal money as an incentive. Yet jails are then filled with these so-called felons, at a huge cost to state and local government.

Other victimless crimes have wasted societal resources and simply make no sense to prosecute, especially in light of the federal, state, and local budget challenges we face. Moreover, too many lawyers are facilitating spurious lawsuits on individuals and businesses. What is compounding these problems is that there are no real penalties for filing frivolous lawsuits (unlike the "loser pays" practice in England). One result is that businesses can be ruined by lawyers bringing lawsuits every time a company stock goes down, someone is injured, or some other perceived harm occurs.

The third role of federal government is to promote the general welfare. This is a laudable challenge for any society, but the promise cannot be unlimited and requires setting standards and priorities. For example, is every American entitled to clean water? That deals with infrastructure. On the other hand, is every American entitled to own a home? This view, aggressively pushed by politicians onto federal regulators, led to the sub-prime mortgage debacle, which almost collapsed the American and global financial systems.

In other guises, promoting the general welfare has come to mean universal health care or cradle-to-grave social programs. Indeed, we are paying the price today for unrestrained good intentions. I do believe that government should help its citizens at certain critical times. No American should die from hunger or untreated disease. With notable exceptions (severe disabilities and old age), this aid should be temporary and designed to *incentivize* people to keep trying to improve their lot.

But what about federal spending that doesn't fit into one of these three categories? Again, any additional spending should still be subject to triage and priority setting. Should we subsidize crops that are not healthy for Americans? Should we be laying off teachers and cutting the class size of non–special education students so we can ensure that every special-needs child has personalized education? Should we consider the cost of keeping terminally ill patients alive? The "death panel" accusations as part of the 2009–2010 health-care debate were a deliberate perversion of a commonsense bipartisan effort to compensate doctors for discussing end-of-life options with patients.

I have some personal views about how such analysis and triage should proceed, some of which include the following procedural suggestions:

Identify all government spending by whether it invests in and promotes the future of our children, or is a clearly rational response to a specific, high-priority need. I have previously explained why our nation's future depends on future generations.

Require measurements in all government spending programs to assess whether the program is working, and include triggers to discontinue any program if it is not meeting the goals assumed when it passed Congress. This is mere common sense, even if it prevents politicians from promising all things to all people.

Cut overseas spending unless it promotes a clear strategic priority. Our spending in Afghanistan, Egypt, Iraq, and South Korea is vastly disproportionate to our spending elsewhere, and we need to reallocate resources.

Link the compensation of our federal legislators to our annual national deficit. For example, a bill might be passed that says, "Congressional salaries will be reduced 20 percent from prior year salaries if the budget the Congress approves is not balanced." Such an approach might require a constitutional amendment but is clearly worth such a challenge. And if such a measure seems harsh, remember that this is what happens every day in the business world in one form or another (usually the executives are fired or the business is closed). The simple fact is that politicians are not doing their job by making tough decisions; rather, they take the easy way out by saying "yes" to virtually everything, especially if it gains them campaign contributions.

Require Congress to vote up or down on a bipartisan commission to address our national debt and unfunded liabilities. This actually was a bipartisan proposal in the Senate, defeated in 2010, that would have created a commission to examine all federal taxes and spending. It would have empowered a commission to come up with a balanced budget proposal and required a simple up or down congressional vote on the proposal. A similar approach was taken a few years ago on the contentious issue of which American military bases should be closed. It worked because Congress voted only to accept or reject the conclusions of the commission. The driver is requiring an up or down vote by Congress on a proposal that cannot be amended. Regrettably, President Obama instead created a bipartisan commission whose recommendations Congress will not be required to vote up or down.

POLICY RECOMMENDATIONS

In addition to the above procedural suggestions, I have several specific policy recommendations that I believe are crucial to restoring sanity to our nation's fiscal condition:

Reduce unfunded pension liabilities for public unions. In this regard, I have five specific suggestions:

Immediately freeze all government-defined benefit plans. This means no newly hired workers will benefit from the plans.

They should be eligible for defined-contribution 401(k) or 403(b) plans, which means you pay for these plans as you go.

Stop all consideration of any "card check" bills. If enacted into law, the so-called Employee Free Choice Act will allow secret unionization and thus destroy the ability of employers to control their pension costs.

Stop requiring that federal government money go only to those using union labor. This provision is what the Democrats in Congress try to put in every stimulus and jobs bill (under the euphemism of requiring government to pay a "prevailing wage"). This not only raises the taxpayers' cost of government programs but also expands unfunded defined benefit obligations.

Stop "in-sourcing" government work. The recent Obama Administration initiative to shift work from private employers to government has been executed with questionable ethics and does not consider the enormously higher future costs of using government workers and the overhead that supports them.

Rescind local, state, and federal government-defined benefit plan obligations to unions as the sponsoring localities declare bankruptcy. This is unpleasant and unfair to those that have worked careers with a promised pension, but employees are creditors like everyone else, and unlike the pre-packaged GM bankruptcy, we cannot throw over all other creditors in favor of one class. Yes, it is most unfortunate that we must focus on the benefits of long-tenured employees, but as our nation's fiscal woes dramatically mount because of spending promiscuity, we must make tough decisions.

Reduce Social Security spending. The social security obligation is financially choking our nation, and soon we will have very few workers supporting an aging population that is living longer and longer. Fortunately, we have difficult but straightforward solutions. First, we must raise the retirement age before payments are made. Second, we need to means-test the payments to recipients. Third, we must stop automatic cost-of-living increases. Although these break the "contract" for some contributors, we can no longer let our older generation steal from the younger generation.

Cut Medicare and Medicaid spending. Most importantly, we must do the following:

▸ Reform medical malpractice costs and incentives. Simply by limiting jury awards in malpractice cases, we would save $54 billion over the next ten years according to the Congressional Budget Office. If doctors' malpractice premiums can be lowered, if they are not discouraged from practicing defensive medicine, and if they can spend their time outside a courtroom, then their reimbursements can be slowed because their costs don't have to be raised.

▸ Reconsider end-of-life treatment policies. The last few months of life's treatment is estimated to consume one-third to one-half of all health-care costs. To address this problem, when getting a driver's license every American should be asked to state his or her preferences for end-of-life care. More provocatively, a person could choose to forgo end-of-life non-palliative care in return for a cash payment from the government, which could be given to the heirs. The issue is not the falsely named "death panels" but rather free choice by Americans when they still have the capacity to make the choice.

► Reward innovation that cuts costs and/or improves health. Drug companies are now incentivized to develop and test variations of drugs to extend expiring patents. Such drugs often provide only marginally improved benefits. Instead, every treatment must be measured relative to its cost and the benefit it confers. Further, doctors and drug companies that develop game-changing drugs and treatments should be recognized and rewarded.

► Reward and encourage healthy lifestyles. With two-thirds of Americans overweight or obese, and with "lifestyle" choices contributing to the bulk of American health-care costs, from diabetes to low infant birth weights, this is a realm of potentially great savings. First Lady Michelle Obama is right to focus on childhood obesity. Its societal cost is huge.

I should note that the 2009 and 2010 congressional debate about health care was disingenuous about solutions and actual budgetary impact of the so-called "reform." The "scoring" of the law was deceptive on many levels: It assumed six years of expense compared to ten years of revenue. It assumed a 21 percent cut in physician Medicare reimbursement, which was immediately restored in May 2010. It assumed $350 billion in "unspecified" Medicare cuts. It did not even include the $100 billion it will cost the federal government to operate the program. We cannot tolerate such deception by our politicians.

Capture "off the book" tax revenues. The fact is that a large portion of Americans escape paying taxes because they don't report their true income. The IRS estimates that the cash economy forces the government to lose some $300 billion annually in lost taxes, which of course imposes a higher tax burden on everyone else. Don't believe me? Run a free ad on Craigslist for any non-skilled job from waiter to nanny, and see how many responses you get from people who insist on being paid off the books. When my wife and I hired a nanny, most experienced candidates insisted on off-the-books payments because that was what they had done before in their economic interests. Sadly for them, they received no benefit from the Social Security match that the law requires the rest of us to pay (7.5 percent of their salary), and they built up no Social Security benefits; however, they also pay no income taxes. Among those we need to capture:

► From the working poor: Many of those reaping government benefits are doing so because they are not reporting all their income and so qualify as "needy." The Las Vegas doorman getting fistfuls of dollars, the maids, bellboys, hairdressers, cab and limo drivers, bartenders, and others getting tips and income by conducting a cash business are certainly entitled to the tips and other income that they receive. But they are not entitled to pay no taxes on this income. Movement to electronic payments will ease tax under-reporting and help keep people honest. In addition to the tens of billions of legitimate payments going to the IRS, we should see a drop-off in eligibility for government assistance programs and thus lower expenditures for these programs.

But it is not only the tax revenue that is lost, it is the benefits that are obtained fraudulently by those claiming poverty. Anyone seeking government payments should have a high barrier to prove that they are entitled to the payments and are reporting all the money they make. Given the fact that most low-wage earners pay little taxes on reported income—and actually get money back through the Earned Income Credit—there is little reason not to insist that everyone be paid "on the books." Absent this change, the Earned Income Credit should be eliminated because it is rife with and encourages fraud. Moreover, it is only right that every citizen pays legally required taxes. Yet today, barely a majority of adult Americans actually pay income taxes.

▶ From small businesses: Many small businesses operate with two sets of books so that they will never show a profit for tax purposes. Most commonly, many personal expenses are attributed to the business and thus are tax-deductible. That is unfair even if it is how business is done in this country, and a few thousand comprehensive audits of small businesses would uncover patterns and trends useful in tax collection. I am concerned that small businesses are over-regulated, but running a party store or nail salon should not be a tool for tax avoidance.

▶ From credit card companies and large companies and their fraudulent executive expense accounts: Overlooked fraud is not restricted to the working poor and small businesses. Some executives at larger companies take advantage of the generous cash rebate programs from credit card companies to transfer corporate expense payments into certificates usable like cash for personal expenses at restaurants and retailers. One former employee at CEA used a corporate American Express card to pay company bills and to accumulate "points," which he said would be used for last-minute business air travel. When I asked him to account for the benefits, I learned that, for the $3 million in American Express corporate purchases he'd made over eighteen months, he had received $30,000 in cash equivalencies at clothing stores and restaurants. He was immediately fired, but he probably never paid taxes on that $30,000 he stole from us. Credit card companies should be held accountable for these gifts. Comprehensive category audits are needed, and penalties for willful fraud need to be increased. For example, the IRS should simply subpoena the top 10,000 gift certificate receivers from American Express to determine how their cash equivalencies were used. Were they used for personal or corporate expenses? If it was corporate spending that "earned" the points (or dollars) and they were used to reduce corporate expenses, that is fine. But if individuals at the companies are receiving personal benefits that they are almost certainly not reporting as income to the IRS, then the IRS must act to prevent fraud and collect fair tax revenues.

On another personal note, any greater effectiveness of tax collecting makes me uncomfortable, but it is fair, necessary, and right. I have had challenges with the IRS, as the IRS sought to assess me additional taxes. Two years in a row my response to the IRS was somehow "lost," and they sought to assess additional penalties. The experience was frustrating, and I felt helpless. Eventually, in each case, I prevailed, and the IRS dropped both cases.

I don't like paying taxes. But I recognize that taxes are the price of living in a free society with a functioning, relevant government. No matter how angry I am at our federal government, I remind myself that paying taxes is not only a civic duty but a privilege, as long as these taxes are fairly raised and prudently spent. Our challenge is to ensure that taxes to support government spending are fair and actually promote our nation's defense, prosperity, and welfare.

12

Private Enterprise: Restoring Our Foundation for Growth

"Some people regard private enterprise as a predatory tiger to be shot. Others look on it as a cow they can milk. Not enough people see it as a healthy horse, pulling a sturdy wagon."

—WINSTON CHURCHILL

To CHURCHILL AND most of our citizens today, it seems obvious that private enterprise is the primary driver of quality economic growth and, at least historically, the preferred source of satisfying careers. Yet there is a seemingly incessant condemnation of private enterprise from certain politicians, union leaders, public intellectuals, lawyers, and the media. This steady drumbeat has fomented a multitude of laws and regulations that are hobbling our economic engine, with no end in sight.

To some critics, private enterprise is synonymous with such pejoratives as "big business," "corporate greed," "fat cats," and similar descriptions that label private enterprise as responsible for oh-so-many ills of our society. Clearly, the world these critics live in is out of whack and divorced from reality. But these critics wield significant political power, so they must be confronted, not ignored or discounted.

Let me be clear. The U.S. has more than 23 million businesses. In any population that large, there unfortunately will be bad actors. But an enlightened electorate and courageous political leadership will not support laws and regulations based on the assumption that the bad guys are the norm. Yet that seems to be what we have come to, and it is past time to correct the political dynamics.

I believe there are four major problems that must be aggressively confronted and successfully resolved if we are to ensure that our legal and regulatory structures are reality-based and promote our free enterprise system:

High corporate income tax rate. The U.S. statutory corporate income tax rate is 35 percent, the second highest among developed nations, behind only Japan. There is no rational economic justification for this high rate, not least because it helps drive businesses abroad in search of economies that better appreciate the economic contributions of business. Instead, arguments for the high tax rate are based on notions of social re-engineering and so-called economic justice.

Moreover, the reality is that businesses do not actually pay income taxes; instead, the economic impacts of tax payments are passed on through the corporation to stockholders in the form of lower investment returns, and to customers in the form of higher prices. Those who demonize private enterprise are engaged in a shell con game. Worse, these high tax rates put U.S. companies at a disadvantage compared to their global competitors.

High tax rates on private enterprise investors. Individuals are taxed on their investment returns as both dividends, taxed at the progressive income tax rate, and capital gains, taxed at a separate rate. A 2004 study by the National Bureau of Economic Research reported that:

> Interest in the role of entrepreneurial entry in innovation raises the question of the extent to which tax policy encourages or discourages entry. We find that, while the level of the marginal tax rate has a negative effect in entrepreneurial entry, the progressivity of the tax also discourages entrepreneurship, and significantly so for some groups of households.[62]

Similarly, in a September 2010 study of capital gains taxes, the American Council on Capital Formation concluded what numerous other studies have also found:

> The bottom line is that any capital gains tax increase is counterproductive to real economic growth. To the contrary, a reduction in the capital gains tax rate would be a pro-growth fiscal stimulus that creates new jobs and new businesses, funds entrepreneurship, reduces the unemployment rate, increases productivity, and in the long run brings in more payroll taxes. In the case of capital gains taxation, less means more.[63]

Those who advocate capital gains taxation are actually engaged in class warfare that penalizes all of us.

Excessive, irrational, and corrupt business regulation. The Competitive Enterprise Institute regularly studies the impact

---

62   Gentry, William M. and R. Glenn Hubbard. "Success Taxes, Entrepreneurial Entry, and Innovation." *Social Science Research Network.* June 2004.

63   Sinai, Allen. "Cap Gains Taxation: Less Means More." *The Wall Street Journal.* September 21, 2010.

of federal government regulations. In a 2007 analysis, it found that 3,900 separate regulations imposed by over fifty federal agencies inflicted an astounding annual cost on our economy of $1.2 trillion (and of course regulations have only increased in the last three years). Note that this analysis does not include the vast number of state-level regulations that undoubtedly would dramatically expand the cost to our society of government regulation.

In that regard, the American Tort Reform Association recently released a study that grades state-level laws on "the good government principles of public disclosure, competitive bidding, oversight and fiscal responsibility. It focuses on the inadequacies of requirements placed on state attorneys general as they sometimes engage in inappropriate relationships with outside counsel." A key conclusion of the study is:

> Some activist state attorneys general are offering no-bid contingency fee contracts, potentially worth many millions of dollars or more, to personal injury lawyers who have made substantial campaign contributions to those same AGs. This abusive pursuit of personal interests directly conflicts with the public interest, and state laws should work to eliminate such abuse.[64]

Regulations increase the time and costs of business activities, including innovation, and often penalize only U.S. firms because foreign firms are beyond the reach of our regulators. There is clearly a set of valid reasons for some types of business regulation, such as for certain matters of consumer health and safety, but in most cases, there is little or

---

64   American Tort Reform Association. "Tort Reform Record: June 2010."

no rational analysis of the costs of regulation compared to the benefits of regulation. And where cost-benefit analyses do occur, they invariably miss the impact of unexpected and unintended consequences of regulation. Instead, regulation is all too often imposed and expanded based solely on non-rational, emotional arguments.

In an earlier chapter, I noted the destructive impact of the 2002 Sarbanes-Oxley Act, which regulates financial reporting by public companies and is inhibiting entrepreneurs from raising growth financing and eventually going public. It is worth another mention because a 2009 study from the National Venture Capital Association calculated that 92 percent of all job growth generated by U.S. public firms occurs after a company goes public. Inhibiting entrepreneurial companies from going public is simply another example of foolish regulation that destroys economic growth and job creation.

Destructive class-action lawsuits. Class-action litigation is the lifeblood of a group of lawyers commonly called trial lawyers (also known as the tort bar and plaintiffs' bar). To describe their pernicious impact, I'll merely quote the findings of a 2005 study by the Cato Institute:

> Since 1930, litigation costs have grown four times faster than the overall economy. Federal class actions tripled over the past ten years. Class actions in state courts ballooned by more than 1,000 percent. The U.S. Chamber of Commerce estimates that the annual cost of the tort system translates into $809 per person—the equivalent of a 5 percent tax on wages. The trial lawyers' share—roughly $40 billion in 2002—was half again larger than the annual revenues of Microsoft or Intel. In 2002 the estimated aggregate cost of the tort system was $233 billion,

according to the actuarial firm Tillinghast-Towers Perrin. That cost represented 2.23 percent of our gross domestic product. Over the next ten years the total "tort tax" will likely be $3.6 trillion.[65]

No fair-minded person disputes holding businesses responsible for actions that injure others, but the trial lawyers have turned our legal system into a massive and expensive farce. I personally have watched companies in California sued because they advertise screen-size in TV sets a few millimeters too large, and I have been appalled at lawsuits aimed at companies whose products merely have an expired patent number as part of their packaging. I have been disgusted by scores of class-action lawsuits where lawyers make money and class holders only get pennies. I have seen hundreds of cases where soulless plaintiffs' lawyers file spurious complaints simply to extort a settlement.

As a side note, there seems to be a growing corrupt confluence of regulation and class-action suits. Case in point is the Financial Accounting Standards Board (FASB), whose mission is to promulgate federal accounting standards. This seems straightforward and unobjectionable. However, the FASB is currently considering mandating that companies account for the *potential* cost of ongoing litigation. As revealed by *The Wall Street Journal*, "supporters insist this is merely about disclosure, but the proposal would hurt investors by offering roadmaps for new litigation and bigger settlements ... [by forcing] companies to divulge snapshot details of ongoing litigation that put investors at greater risk of loss."[66]

---

65   Levy, Robert A. "Do's and Don'ts of Tort Reform." Cato Institute. May 2005.

66   "FASB's Tort Bar Gift." *The Wall Street Journal*. August 18, 2010.

My major suggestions for dealing with these problems are as follows:

Lower or eliminate corporate tax rates. As noted above, corporations are pass-through entities to owners and customers. If we drastically lower—or better yet, eliminate—the corporate tax, the government will still collect its tax revenues from taxes on investors, but we will alleviate one of the causes of our corporations being whipping boys of those who are ill-informed or deceitful.

Allow international revenue to be repatriated to the United States. The U.S. is the only country that taxes revenue from abroad—even though it is also taxed by other countries. So corporations respond by keeping billions in cash and not returning it to the United States. Allowing such revenue to return here at a reduced tax rate would stimulate the economy and add to government revenue. This no-brainer is challenged by Democrats as a corporate tax giveaway.

Require every law passed by Congress to be analyzed for its cost-benefit impact on business operations and the nation's economic growth. This should be fairly straightforward. And if this requirement slows down Congress's legislative process, that's probably a side benefit.

Establish implementation timetables for legislation that impacts business. As I noted in a previous chapter, uncertainty in taxes, regulation, and other government initiatives is a huge impediment to business investment, economic growth, and job creation. One solution might be to impose extended periods for legislation and regulation to take effect, with a multi-year timetable for major changes and no less than a one-year timetable for minor changes. This would alleviate at least some of the uncertainly about legislation and would facilitate businesses investment decision-making.

Change our legal system to "loser pays." Anyone is free to file suit against an individual or institution, but if the suit is without merit, the plaintiff pays no penalty aside from his own legal costs, regardless of how meritless the suit was or how much time and expense the defendant incurred. Instead, simple fairness should require that any plaintiff who loses his case must also pay for at least the defendant's legal costs. That is the system in England, where it demonstrably curbs spurious lawsuits, and it is desperately needed here. It likely would also have the additional benefit of curbing the practice of lawyers taking on clients on a contingency fee basis, wherein they bet a company will settle rather than suffer the enormous cost and time to defend a lawsuit. As a companion measure, we should consider capping the amount of contingency fees paid, both in total and as to the share that goes to the plaintiff's lawyer.

Change the standards of liability from automatic damages to actual demonstrable harm. The Recording Industry Association of America (RIAA) lawyers sued 30,000 Americans because the RIAA got laws passed that allowed downloading kids to be sued even without harm to the RIAA or its members being proven. Similarly, one newsletter publisher makes more money off lawsuits than subscriptions because it embeds Web crawling software, waits for years, and then claims millions of dollars in statutory damages by claiming that each day a copy is made is a technical violation. Our laws now occupy tens of thousands of pages, and lawyers scour them for technical violations and then sue. Real harm has become irrelevant.

Enact a moratorium on all new regulations for the next three years, with an exception for national security and public safety. I am honored to adopt this suggestion from George Schultz (former economist; business school dean; Secretary of Labor, Treasury, and State; and senior business executive), who, along with other accomplished scholars, recently advocated this and other measures to deal with our current economic crisis. They said;

> Going forward, regulations should be transparent and simple, pass rigorous cost-benefit tests, and rely to a maximum extent on market-based incentives instead of command and control. Direct and indirect cost estimates of regulations and subsidies should be published before new regulations are put into law.[67]

My further suggestion is to start eliminating existing regulations that don't meet the same standards.

Neither our Founding Fathers nor Winston Churchill would recognize what we have allowed to happen to degrade our free enterprise system, costing us untold trillions of dollars in direct and foregone economic growth. The time for radical restoration is upon us.

---

67 Boskin, Michael J., John F. Cogan, Allen Meltzer, George P. Schultz, and John B. Taylor. "Principles for Economic Revival." *The Wall Street Journal*. September 16, 2010.

13

Innovation Requires Support of U.S. Companies

COMPETING GLOBALLY

A few years ago I was asked to give a keynote address at a Paris business conference. My topic was on what French companies must do to be competitive. I spoke about taking risks, enabling free trade, building markets, and overall economic development. Without being arrogant, I acknowledged that the rest of the world admires and envies innovative technology in American companies. The United States, after all, is the platinum standard.

Immediately following my remarks, the French Minister of Education spoke and evaluated many of my comments. He said that France wants so much to be like the United States that they will soon require all graduating high school students to learn English and to have basic computing skills. I must admit, I was thrilled to hear this. After such strained Franco-American relations, it was a nice change of pace to hear a foreigner speak so approvingly of my country and its business practices.

However, my delight turned to horror as the next French government official spoke. This was the Subminister of the Numerique

(Internet). She made it clear that the strategy in France and through the European Union would be to use antitrust laws to sue companies with "closed" systems. You didn't have to be a rocket scientist to know she was talking about Apple, Intel, Google, and others. In other words, she was explaining how to use government to undercut America's competitive advantage.

It was an eye-opening moment for me. While I understand other countries' envy, and naturally their inclination to do whatever they can to get a leg up on the United States, I started to wonder how our own government was going to counter such measures. But that's just it. The French really don't need to do a thing because the U.S. government not only refuses to defend but, rather, often leads the attack on our crown-jewel companies.

PROTECTING AMERICAN INNOVATION

Our government, primarily through political appointees seeking to make their mark without concern for consequence, uses ambiguous antitrust standards to investigate and often sue our most innovative companies. These investigations and lawsuits spur other countries to challenge, sue, and shake down America's top companies. If the U.S. government leads the charge, how can we possibly object to other countries following suit?

I first noticed this disturbing trend with Microsoft in the 1990s. Bill Gates's empire had "monopoly" power, so the theory went. Yet Microsoft was a homegrown American success story, which not only created thousands of American millionaires and employed tens of thousands of Americans, but also fundamentally changed how we create, write, edit, present, and share information in our daily lives. Microsoft is an American institution. It improved our productivity and changed the world. More, it became one of our leading and biggest companies almost overnight. Created by societal geeks, as a scrappy innovative company, Microsoft's successful domination parallels the story of the birth and success of our nation.

But success breeds enemies, especially in a democracy like ours. The higher you climb, the more your enemies want to tear you down. It wasn't long before our own government began a relentless attack on Microsoft, spurred, ironically enough, by other countries. The envy Microsoft engendered allowed the politicians to pounce, without concern for all the jobs and wealth Gates's creation had given America.

But leaving aside political advantage, what these attacks meant was cost and a shift of resources for Microsoft. None of the suits ever amounted to anything significant. But tens of millions of dollars and thousands of hours of executive time were spent. Also, Apple, Google, and others succeeded in competing against Microsoft. It's not that Microsoft lost its competitive advantage; it's that the government did so much to distract it and thus help its out-of-the box-thinking competitors.

Of course the cycle continues, and what goes around comes around. In the last few years, Apple, Amazon, Google, eBay, and Facebook have all been accused of becoming too powerful. Intel and Qualcomm have been threatened by our government. In Intel's case, the Federal Trade Commission actually demanded that every future product of Intel's be licensed to anyone who wants it.

In the great American novel *Atlas Shrugged*, Libertarian author Ayn Rand fantasized that the country's innovators decide to stop creating in response to our government's determination to punish success. I know firsthand that many of our nation's CEOs are perplexed about our government's irrational desire to punish, demonize, and tax their success. In the real world of business, this surely encourages them to relocate their people, facilities, and perhaps even their headquarters.

As a matter of policy, our government must protect and advocate for leading U.S. companies. This does not mean defending egregious conduct; it means giving American companies the benefit of the doubt. It also means thoughtful policies on taxes, unions, litigation, and resolution to encourage investment, innovation, and jobs.

Innovation requires that potential entrepreneurs trust that government will not punish them for success. A political attack on our best companies should be met with national condemnation. Furthermore, innovation requires a tax system that rewards investment, start-ups, and risk. Taxes should be stable and not subject to changing political winds. Instability in taxation (or in government) causes uncertainty, and uncertainty discourages investment. Innovation requires a certain level of confidence in government.

Innovation does not require that government determine or decide where innovation occurs. It can't, and when it tries, it usually fails, notable exceptions notwithstanding. Our atomic development during World War II and President Kennedy's moon shot were rare cases where government was on the forefront of innovation. But, lest we forget, both occurred during times of great national security challenges: winning a war and defeating the Soviets. We can't depend on national crises to advance innovation. I would hope that the evidence I've presented in this book proves that innovation occurs *despite* government action.

Moreover, innovation does not require massive government spending on entrepreneurs. Innovation does not actually even require a healthy economy. In fact, recession economies often force innovation in companies and by under-employed people or people out of work. Microsoft began in the terrible economy of the late 1970s. For all that the dot-com bubble burst the expectation of instant success, most of today's top Internet companies were created in that time. Sometimes when a company's survival is at risk or a person is unemployed, there is a special focus on doing things differently and undertaking risk. In short, risk is more likely to occur if there is less to lose and more to gain.

At the same time, economic turmoil most often brings out the voices of government intervention. Today, we hear many people advocate that the government should be choosing specific industries for government favor and investment. They argue that government support will help these industries succeed. In some cases that might be true. Government support provides advantages to certain industries, such as the electric vehicle industry and corn farmers producing ethanol.

The problem is that even if you take the billions of dollars of taxpayer support for a particular industry and then you add in the success stories, it's a net loss for our economy because those investment or subsidy dollars from governments are taken from other productive businesses or Americans.

The simple fact is that bureaucrats don't know what will be successful and what won't. The U.S. government has poured billions into ethanol subsidies, and yet ethanol remains a terrible alternative fuel. The U.S. government subsidy policy is also viewed worldwide as causing huge increases in food prices and contributing to massive starvation. But with the farm lobby in Washington, combined with well-intentioned but misguided environmentalists, we are going to have ethanol subsidies for the foreseeable future.

THE RUSH TO SPEND MONEY

Much of the nearly $1 trillion in "stimulus" money went to various industrial investments. In this case, the government quickly decided that it was worth borrowing taxpayer funds to invest strategically in certain industries. Why no one stopped to ask how it could be strategic to rush through billions of dollars in investments, without hearings, consideration of alternatives, objective standards, or anything resembling a reasonable process, seems like a terrible business strategy. Rather the billions were committed without regard to process but with a large regard to politics and contributions. One major industry lobbyist told me that he was amazed that Congress had given his industry billions of dollars—everything he had asked for!

That's what happens when politicians make decisions interfering with the competitive free marketplace: Politics trumps economics.

If there is any doubt as to whether this hurried strategy makes sense, consider the funding obtained by one company from the stimulus package. From this government generosity, one struggling electric car company, Tesla, received $465 million in loans backed by the federal government. Created in 2003 in Palo Alto, California, Tesla had undergone internal management changes but had promised delivery of an electric family sedan for $57,400 (reduced by federal tax credits to American buyers to $49,900). Tesla claimed in mid-2010 that over 2,000 of these cars had been pre-ordered.

The *New York Times* reported in July 2010 that the ambitious claims for the car's performance had yet to be proven with a prototype model. Indeed, if the performance claims were true, some wondered why government funding was even necessary. But the owners and early backers were enthusiastic. Not surprisingly, many of the funders also provided political funding to Democratic politicians. According to the SEC, Tesla produces *fifteen* cars per week—hardly a winning business model.

The process of the funding and the amount of funding can and will result in massive amounts of wasted taxpayer dollars. I will never forget a meeting I had in 2009 with a senior government official whose responsibility was to oversee billions in stimulus spending on broadband use. Under the stimulus package, he had to assess the population and then dole out funding to "underserved" areas.

Consistent with this charge, he had quickly entered separate contracts with entities in each state and had committed over $100 million in government funding for contracts with state entities. In the summer of 2009, after making this $100-million commitment, he met with executives from a company that could have easily gathered this information and given it to the government for a tiny fraction of the $100 million the government was spending.

The official was at first thrilled to see how easily the data was available and told me that it was the "most important" meeting he'd had as a government official. But I guess he soon realized that he could not get out of paying those $100 million in contracts. Over $100 million in taxpayer money was wasted simply because of a rush to spend. All this money went to groups each seeking their own piece of the government pie and each using registered or unregistered lobbyists.

LOBBYING FOR AMERICA

Our nation's capital is overrun with lobbyists, and most are seeking special favors or money from government. I gave some statistics about D.C. lobbyists and lawyers at the beginning of this book, but they bear repeating here. More than 10,000 lobbyists are formally registered to lobby the federal government (and this certainly understates the number who lobby but do not meet the 20 percent lobbying threshold before formal filing is required). Interest groups—including unions, businesses, and the AARP—reported spending $3.5 billion to influence the federal government in 2009, and likely a higher amount will be reported for 2010.

American Bar Association statistics reveal that the number of "active, resident" lawyers in Washington, D.C., jumped from 46,689 in 2008 to 48,456 in 2009. This is the second highest increase in the nation, with only New York adding more lawyers. Washington, D.C., has one lawyer for every twelve citizens!

Why the large increase in lawyers and lobbying? Because the more government gets involved in business, the more protections businesses need to save them from government. The Obama Administration and Congress have been legislating and regulating to a degree never seen before in most of our lives. This has fueled the Washington economy. And the Washington boom will continue as the federal government hires thousands of new employees to meet the mandates of the health care and financial "reform" bills.

Business owners who create jobs are frustrated. They don't understand why Washington is making life more difficult for them. They are perplexed with new requirements, like the health-care law mandating that every business must report to the IRS any information on any purchase exceeding $600. They see all sorts of federal payroll taxes rising, and they don't understand why American corporate taxes are the second highest in the developed world.

National business leaders agree that industry has been hurt by the well-meaning efforts of the federal government to help the economy. Heap on threats of tax increases, new rules, an increasingly restrictive union agenda, and a protectionist environment, and you get job creators who view the federal government's recent activism as harmful. An anti–free market and anti-employer environment has industries looking at overseas investments for growth. Business executives from large and small companies view the United States as an increasingly hostile place to do business.

The lack of business confidence, investment, and job creation are not surprising given how our political leaders have demonized the very businesses whose investment, profits, and growth create jobs. The word "corporate" is too often combined with the word "greed." Profits are considered evil or excessive. The "free market" has shifted from a positive description of the American economic system to a pejorative. The "invisible hand" of the free market is being replaced entirely by a visible hand of what politicians think a market should look like.

Our American edge in entrepreneurial activity and innovation is threatened by our own government. New burdens and taxes are being added without considering real business and job creation implications.

GOOD GOVERNMENT

Government's role in innovation is important, but limited. At best, it adjusts the legal framework to allow new innovations to flourish; at worst, it puts up roadblocks to protect older industries. For example, in 1996 Jim Gilmore, a bright, principled Jeffersonian conservative, was elected Virginia's governor based on a simple eight-letter promise: "No Car Tax." Although he kept his promise to cut the much-hated tax on cars, his bigger achievement is that he made Virginia the leader in fostering innovation by creating a legal framework for business to be done over the Internet.

Virginia's legal revolution was engineered by Don Upson, whom Governor Gilmore installed as Virginia's (and the world's) first Secretary of Technology. Don had a vision. With a background working for technology companies and for a congressional committee focused on making government work better, Don believed that the Internet fundamentally changed everything, but that Internet innovation was constrained by old laws requiring hard copies and signatures to do business.

To help lay the groundwork for a technology-friendly state, Don created a bipartisan commission charged with finding ways for Virginia to embrace the Internet and innovation. The commission included visionary and respected legislators from both parties as well as leading tech luminaries like AOL founder Steve Case. It also included well-known Indian immigrant entrepreneur Sudhakar Shenoy. While serving on the commission, I met and befriended Sudhakar and became convinced that we needed more great Americans like him. Patriotic, effusive, and brilliant, Sudhakar's IT company employed hundreds of Americans. He always had business ideas, and he relished connecting people and supporting local charities.

With Don's vision and the inspired leadership of the prestigious group of business leaders, the commission agreed to propose changes to Virginia law that allowed the Internet to grow and serve as a basis for transacting business. For example, e-mail could serve as legal notice, electronic signatures could be valid, and exchange of electronic copies could create a binding contract.

The state legislature quickly turned these proposals into law, and others noticed. Egyptian president Hosni Mubarak made a special trip to Virginia to learn about the state's approach to the Internet. I was honored to explain to him the perspective from the consumer technology industry. We also visited Egypt and other countries to discuss Virginia's unique focus on the Internet as a business enabler.

The Virginia experience taught me that a bipartisan effort with industry participation can move innovation forward. No special handouts or competitive advantage—simply a diversity of citizens and smart legislators helping move forward a basic government function, a legal framework to create and enforce contracts. With the strategy and vision of real leaders like Don Upson, government moved quickly into the Internet Age. Don is a true hero of technology.

Government has a role to play in helping America's innovative companies. It's a specific role that should not be focused on picking winners and losers. Innovation, like water, will find its own level, if it's allowed to flourish. Here are some specific suggestions:

Clarify the ambiguous "monopolization" antitrust standards.
The EU is determined to gain a competitive advantage over the United States by suing successful American tech companies. The federal government should resist these efforts and not be complicit in destroying our companies. Establishing a more coherent "monopoly" antitrust standard will help clarify when and where the U.S. government should be protecting U.S. companies. Indeed, Edwin S. Rockefeller, the former chairman of the American Bar Association's section of antitrust law, recently suggested that antitrust is "unsound as economics" and "gives government officials the power to interfere whimsically with freedom of contract, frequently on behalf of losers."[68]

Defend American companies internationally as a matter of national interest. When the EU props up Airbus to gain an advantage over Boeing, the U.S. government should be the first objector. I'm not against our government or our companies handing out contracts to foreign companies—if it's a better price and a better product, that's the way the game is played. What I'm against is when our government does nothing, or actively participates, when a foreign government gives its companies a competitive advantage.

Change visa and citizenship policies so leading American companies can employ the world's best and brightest here in America.
I discussed the importance of changing our immigration laws in a previous chapter, but I can't stress enough how invaluable bringing foreign talent is to American innovation. Immi-

---

68   Rockefeller, Edwin S. "Time for Anitrust to Bite the Dust." *The Wall Street Journal.* August 19, 2010.

grants build companies, they add to our economic growth, and they are an integral part of our innovation strategy. We need to refine the laws so that, instead of "outsourcing" our talent, we are bringing it here. As it is, our rules today encourage U.S. companies to open up foreign facilities.

14

Innovation Requires a National Energy Policy

OUR ADDICTION

By now, I hope that my policy prescriptions to promote and advance innovation will inoculate us from charges of arguing for expansive government, "living" constitutional theory, and redistribution of wealth. In other words, I believe in smaller government and a return to constitutional principles of liberty, but that does not mean we cannot view our current energy consumption as dangerous and create a national strategy to discover alternative fuel sources. This isn't about ideology. It's about securing our energy future, and that future is with less oil imported from overseas.

The fact is, many of our international challenges stem from what President Bush called "our addiction to oil." Now, we should always bring a level of skepticism when politicians start talking about ending our addiction to oil. If memory serves, the line was first raised in the Carter Administration, when I was a young man, and I'm still filling my car with petroleum-based fuel. It's a tired cliché, but we made it to the moon in a third of the time that has passed since President Carter talked about getting the nation off oil.

In the ensuing years, we've had to endure various attempts to get rid of our addiction. Of course, none have worked. We've had attempts to promote electric, ethanol, and solar power, to name but a few. These aren't "pet rock"–style technologies, but they have had thirty years to prove themselves and have come up short. Which isn't to say that they aren't the future. But the reason they haven't worked is because we haven't had a firm strategy and a committed government to make them work.

This requires more than government subsidies. Subsidies are what you give when you're pretty sure what you're subsidizing isn't a real industry. It's like our ethanol subsidies. But the further we get toward the critical moment when the world's oil resources dwindle and oil prices increase, the further we get to America's fall. Our energy needs require oil. The United States consumes more than twice as much oil as the next most consuming nation (China). When the spigot runs dry, we will be in a world of hurt. We have mistakenly come to assume that we'll figure out something when it's urgent. As Winston Churchill once supposedly remarked (insultingly, but also approvingly), "You can always count on Americans to do the right thing—after they've tried everything else."

Now this might be true. But we seem to have taken Sir Winston's summation too much to heart. As Americans, we like to think that, in the end, we'll figure it out. We have before; we will again. As much as our history bears this out, we should also consider the exceptions to the rule. Slavery? We had eighty years to figure that out, and when we finally got around to it, we nearly destroyed ourselves. Our position before World War II? We were dangerously ill prepared to fight a technologically advanced enemy, never mind two at the same time. We know the end, so it's hard to appreciate just how precarious our situation was in early 1942. We had no serviceable Navy (destroyed at Pearl Harbor), we had terrible tanks, and we could barely muster a decent army (read about our travails in Northern Africa).

In both cases, we prevailed, but by the skin of our teeth. As Wellington said of Waterloo, it was a close run thing. I think we'd rather have not fought the Civil War to end slavery nor seen so many American lives lost in World War II before we figured out how to fight a war.

In any case, we are nearing the point in our energy needs where doing nothing is no longer acceptable. Our concern with the Middle East is in part a result of our dependence on its largest export. If you don't agree, ask yourself why we aren't as concerned with the devastation of Africa. The whole continent is destroying itself, yet somehow Africa's concerns aren't in our national interest. Now it's not just the United States that is obsessed with the Middle East; the rest of the civilized world depends on the oil as well. But that's why it's our time to lead.

The reality is that our dependence on foreign oil is an economic concern, it's a national security concern, and it's an innovation concern. We must cut our reliance on overseas oil for at least three reasons: economics, foreign policy, and innovation.

The first reason is economic. Every dollar we spend on overseas oil is a dollar of outflow not supporting American business or jobs. This outflow of currency without creation of U.S. jobs is harmful to our nation. Like the newspaper industry, the oil consumption industry uses an outmoded business model. Technologically speaking, it's inefficient to find, produce, and deliver oil, especially when we know how to get energy by more direct, if not economic, means.

Second, our reliance on imported oil affects our foreign policy. It's come to the point where this assertion is no longer a partisan issue. In his 2008 bid for the presidency, John McCain railed against our dependence on overseas oil. Congressional Republicans rail against it today. No one thinks that to have an economy entirely dependent on a volatile region of the world is good policy. It's like having your supply source at the edge of Niagara Falls.

The third reason is for innovation. In a previous chapter, I mentioned the atomic bomb and the moon shot policies of the United States. Of course, I mentioned them as exceptions to the rule that government can't promote innovation. But I also said that both those attempts were done in times of national crisis, and that helped spur a very rare successful collusion of government and the private sector. We are in such a moment with energy today. With a national commitment to rid ourselves of oil dependency, the private sector can and will find alternatives. But we need to be smart about it.

Relying on fuel-efficiency mandates on car companies and unrealistic assumptions about renewable sources of energy is not a strategy. It's a halfhearted attempt by politicians to prop up a donor industry or generate good headlines. It's uncoordinated, it's unsophisticated, and it's unrealistic. Putting pressure on American companies, such as with cap-and-trade mandates, is a recipe for disaster. It punishes instead of promotes.

However, we can eliminate reliance on overseas oil by 2025 by taking concrete steps:

The president must challenge Americans. This is the man-on-the-moon challenge that Kennedy issued. We need a deadline, and we need a national plan to get us there, with measurable deliverables and consequences for failure. The president should follow up by announcing that each state's oil usage will be measured and that those with the highest percentage drops will be recognized and rewarded

We must build new nuclear power plants. We need more electricity: estimates for usage of many hybrid and electric cars assume a stable electricity source. If France can get 80 percent of its power from nuclear, so can we. The anti-nuclear movement, which unfortunately still holds sway in Washington, is based on thirty-year-old presumptions and spectacular failures, like Three Mile Island and Chernobyl. Nuclear energy is safe, carbon-neutral, and cheap, when we get the plants built. But our regulatory process is designed to delay and impose huge costs on every new nuclear project. The U.S. process takes decades, and has crippled our nuclear industry. Japan, Korea, France, and others have much shorter planning and construction cycles.

We must continue to pursue renewable energy sources but be realistic in our estimates. Solar, wind, and saw grass are nice, but their ability to replace existing energy sources has been exaggerated. We should still encourage their development through tax benefits, but we need an honest assessment of their potential to help us set realistic goals.

We must incentivize Americans to buy cars that use less gas. I'm not generally in favor of higher taxes just because if you want less of something you tax it. But that's why it makes sense to institute a higher gas tax. This is only punitive if you drive a gas guzzler. Gasoline taxes should be increased five cents every six months for the foreseeable future. This will encourage Americans to consider fuel efficiency in their car purchases over the long term. It will also influence where they choose to live over the long term. Proceeds from the gas tax should be invested in alternative fuel source technologies and in infrastructure. The anti-tax brigade should recall that President Reagan raised the gas tax to pay for infrastructure.

We must encourage people to move closer to their jobs. My company offers any employee $25,000 if the employee buys a home in the county where we are located. The purpose of the program is to save energy, to get our employees to spend less time commuting, and to establish loyalty. The $25,000 is in the form of a three-year, forgivable loan. Even without the tax benefits, the program is successful and appreciated, and a good recruiting tool to attract employees. Imagine if this loan were tax-free income—many people would move closer to their jobs. Plus real estate agents would be quite busy.

We must encourage telework. Not every employer has jobs amenable to telework, but many jobs are, and they should be encouraged. This means formal programs, restricting employer liability, providing the equipment and tools, and deploying broadband and leadership at the top. Major weather events such as snowstorms have proven that many employees can and should be encouraged to spend some time working from home.

15

An Innovation Lesson in Health Care

PRIVATE INNOVATION

Jim Traficant was undergoing his second liver transplant when the thought struck him, *There has to be a better way.* He had had a fast recovery following the procedure, but it wasn't long before complications arose: His body was rejecting the new liver. He was rushed back to the hospital, where he remained for a month and was kept alive with expensive life-threatening treatments.

When he got home, the rejection happened again. He repeated his ordeal once more. After another month in the hospital, where he was treated with experimental medication, Jim returned home and began to study his medication and blood work results. This led to a breakthrough. He was able to identify an algorithm that could predict when rejection would occur. When his body rejected the transplant a third time, Jim was prepared. Based on the results of his work, Jim was able to avoid another hospital stay with the proper medication.

The better way Jim realized was in the data—the health information. It was the key to proper medical treatment. What astonished

Jim was that his doctors weren't so much interested in the data as they were interested in treating the problems that arose. In other words, Jim's treatment was reactive rather than proactive.

This didn't make any sense to him. He knew there were reams of data on his condition and on others like him. Why couldn't we use that data, as a physicist uses equations, to predict a future event? Jim wanted to find a way to put the "science" back in medical science. For too long, he felt, medicine has behaved more like an art: You feel your way around until you hit upon the solution. That might work for a painter or writer, but it doesn't work when lives are on the line. As many as 98,000 Americans die each year as result of medical errors, with up to 7,000 of these deaths attributed to adverse drug events from medication errors. That's a crisis, and Jim was determined not to allow himself to become another statistic.

These days Jim Traficant is the vice president of Harris Corporation's Health Care Solutions business. One of Harris's principal projects is developing the CONNECT system, which is an open-source software that allows health-care providers to exchange patient information seamlessly. It acts much like a Wikipedia page—connecting your information to every other conceivable page of relevant information. The U.S. government has incorporated CONNECT in many of its departments, such as the Social Security Administration and the Department of Veteran Affairs, to establish interoperability between agencies and to improve care. This all resulted from Jim's insistence as a patient on the edge of life: there had to be a better way.

If I could think of a credo for innovation, I probably couldn't do better than that: Finding a better way is the heart of innovation. It's recognizing a need, knowing the tools at your disposal, and *creating* that better way. Jim found a better way, and today thousands of patients are better off because Jim wasn't willing to accept the status quo.

And now CONNECT is revolutionizing the way we think about health care. It's lowering costs and improving patient care, leading to fewer medical error fatalities. That's innovation at its best.

GOVERNMENT INTERVENTION

But there's a flip side to this health-care coin. The Obama administration's health-care reform law made greater interoperability between government agencies a priority. It has helped establish CONNECT as the gateway to reforming our entire health-care system—for the better. But the law is also a classic example of the government trying—and failing—to use government as a stand-in for the free market.

For instance, the government cannot reduce costs—in any industry—without having prices rise somewhere else. Only the free market can do that. But that's not my biggest beef with Obamacare. Rather, my concern begins with how this whole bill of pie-in-the-sky promises was created in the first place.

What all Americans should be upset about is how both parties turned an appropriate national debate on the health of Americans into a unregulated scrum in which brute force, deception, and back-room politics resulted in bad legislation. The absence of real substantive discussion or any attempt to agree on the facts led to the party-line passage of a huge, little-understood spending program.

First, calling it health-care "reform" was totally deceptive. The bill's focus was obtaining coverage for working poor Americans who do not presently have health-care coverage. Most of the bill prescribed a method of defining the coverage and then imagining creative ways of paying for it.

Second, a central premise of the debate was that somehow Americans now have inferior health care compared to the rest of the Western world. Statistics on infant mortality, birth weight, and life expectancy were used to "prove" that Americans paid more for health coverage but got less in return. Yet those statistics say more about American society than they do about American health care. Compared to the rest of the developed world, more underage women have babies in the United States; compared to the rest of the developed world, Americans are fatter. While we can regret these facts, we cannot say they are the result of America's inferior health-care system, so using them to argue for health-care reform is disingenuous. These are lifestyle choices that American make, and they cannot and should not be viewed as caused by the health-care system.

In fact, by measures that don't consider lifestyle, such as cancer detection and cure rates for most diseases, the United States is the best nation in the world for health care. There is a reason the world's wealthiest individuals with life-threatening diseases flock to the U.S. for treatment: We have the most successful and innovative treatments. So the premise of "reforming" health care was flawed.

Third, the debate was most memorable for its lack of facts. In July 2009, President Obama charged that a surgeon gets paid $50,000 for a leg amputation. In fact, as the American College of Surgeons pointed out the next day that Medicare pays a surgeon between $740 and $1,140 for a leg amputation. This payment also includes the evaluation of the patient on the day of the operation and patient follow-up care that is provided for ninety days after the operation.[69]

The College noted that this wasn't the first untrue comment by the president:

The President suggested that a surgeon's decision to remove a

---

69   American College of Surgeons. "Statement from the American College of Surgeons Regarding Recent Comments from President Obama." August 12, 2009.

child's tonsils is based on the desire to make a lot of money. That remark was ill-informed and dangerous, and we were dismayed by this characterization of the work surgeons do. Surgeons make decisions about recommending operations based on what's right for the patient.

But if the president was overzealous in his efforts to get his signature bill passed, the debate in Congress was worse. Based on an offhand comment by Sarah Palin about "death panels," the Republicans made that a unifying description of the health-care bill. Yet the only relevant phrase Republicans could point to in the legislation was a provision, originally supported by many key Republicans, that compensated doctors for talking with patients about all their end-of-life options.

Anyone who has dealt with a terminally ill relative or friend and gone through this process understands that it is an excruciating time and that doctors play a vital role in carefully and sensitively describing the options. Nonetheless, this somehow became the provision that Republicans pointed to as allowing "death panels" and became the primary argument for their opposition to the bill.

A much more important, but little noticed and discussed, provision in the bill effectively imposes some type of rationing of Medicare by a panel of unelected Americans. This huge cut in reimbursements to doctors without any specifications, guidance, or criteria gives a few unelected Americans enormous authority to effectively cut $350 billion in funding for various treatments in medicine that they perceive as too costly, unnecessary, or ineffective. This little-discussed provision in the legislation, if not reversed by a later Congress, means that doctors who want to use certain forms of treatment for a specific patient's needs may be paid little or nothing at all.

THE COST OF GOVERNMENT INTERVENTION

The final 2,000-page bill was drafted by a handful of lawmakers behind closed doors and not shared with members of Congress until hours before the House vote. But something was happening across the country. Democratic lawmakers found themselves confronted by angry constituents at town hall meetings, upset at the bill's soaring cost. The constituent uprising and Tea Party protests were so alarming that many Democratic members said they could not support the bill if it expanded the federal deficit.

Thus for the Democratic House leadership, the March 2010 vote hinged on their ability to claim significant deficit savings. Days before the House vote, the leadership announced that the supposedly "nonpartisan" Congressional Budget Office (CBO) had scored the legislation and had said the bill would result in $100 billion in savings over the next ten years.

But to score the bill, the CBO was given a set of assumptions provided by the Democrats and the Obama Administration. So less than a month after the bill was signed into law, the CBO quietly acknowledged that it had understated by at least $115 billion the cost of the health-care bill. The CBO also explained that its scoring did not include fifty-two items that had no specific funding level but that the law said should be given "such sums as may be necessary."

Since the initial CBO scoring, I questioned whether the government scorekeepers were candid in saying the health-care bill would reduce the budget deficit. In April 2010, I publically challenged Dr. Peter Orszag, then director of the Office of Management and Budget, on this when he spoke at the Economic Club of Washington.

It turns out that those of us who expressed skepticism on the health-care bill's deficit-reducing qualities were right. Although one always appreciates vindication, it doesn't change the fact that the health-care bill passed based on a huge and fraudulent deception aimed at the American people.

Yet the health-care deficit fraud continued. While running for Congress in the Fall of 2010, Democratic Representative Jim Moran of Virginia produced a glossy brochure that defended his vote on bill as "reducing the federal deficit by more than $100 billion over the next decade." He cited the House Budget Committee as his source. Apparently, unlike the CBO, the House Budget Committee saw no need to correct its errors.

Despite the CBO correction, as of November 2010, if you went to the White House Web site you would still have seen the fiction that the health-care law would "reduce the deficit by $100 billion over the next ten years."

In fact, the health-care law will not only explode the federal deficit, it will impose huge new costs on states that must pay for creation of insurance pools and the processing of the estimated 16 million additional Americans to the expanded Medicaid program. Moreover, the law puts an increasing amount of the Medicaid burden on the states. These new costs are a growing concern in state capitols.

Should it matter that the new health-care law may raise our federal and state deficits by at least $2 trillion more than promised? Yes. Five percent annual interest on $2 trillion is $100 billion. That means our kids will have to pony up roughly $100 billion each year just to finance the new costs from this bill. With states already in serious fiscal trouble and some cutting school to four-day weeks, this new burden forces us to confront a rather scary future of inflation, choking taxes, cuts in services, and a declining economy.

If the public had known the true cost of health-care reform before our political leaders sought the rushed and fixed CBO scoring, then we would have had a different outcome. If political leaders from both sides had tried to define the problem, which was originally about millions of underinsured Americans, had agreed on the facts, and had debated different solutions and their true costs, we would have had a more intelligent discussion and a much better result. Maybe we could have had malpractice litigation reform as part of the law, which would save about $40 billion in spending, according to the CBO.

Some proponents of the bill explain these deliberate deceptions through the old adage "the ends justify the means." In fact, then–House Speaker Nancy Pelosi, in a rather unguarded moment, said that we would have to pass the bill to find out what's in it. This Machiavellian logic eliminated any chance for cost-effective improvements in health-care coverage, which a reasoned examination of the facts would have aided.

Sooner or later our nation is going to have to address our serious budget crisis. It will require tough decisions, compromises, and, above all, an adherence to facts. Americans deserve the truth. Sadly, they did not get it in the health-care debate.

WHAT SHOULD HAVE HAPPENED WITH THE HEALTH-CARE DEBATE IF INNOVATION MATTERED? THE TECHNOLOGY INDUSTRY PROVIDES SOME LESSONS.

The consumer technology industry is defined by rapid innovation and falling prices. Its success has allowed content creators, service providers, Web sites, blogs, and all sorts of new media to flourish. It is intensely competitive and yet loved by consumers. This fast moving, deflationary, job-creating, $160-billion industry has several basic tenets that all participants understand. These principles are relevant to the health-care debate.

1. Competition produces better products and lower prices. Consumer electronics is an intensively competitive, low-margin business. Companies succeed by innovation, quality, reputation, and efficiency. With the advent of the Internet, consumers are better informed than ever about the quality of their products.

Lesson for policy makers: Competition requires consumer choice and information. Consumer insurance choice is limited as companies are artificially restricted from competing across state lines. Consumers have little incentive to be smart purchasers when someone else is paying—many doctors see patients flood their offices once their deductibles are met. Consumers should not be ordering from a menu without prices: they should always pay a portion of their health-care costs. As in the rest of the economy, there is no such thing as a free lunch.

2. Innovation is rewarded. The first to market takes big risks but also sees gains in sales, reputation, and market share. Failure is considered a learning experience.

Lesson for policy makers: The proposals debated ignored the risks and costs imposed on health-care providers (malpractice litigation, for example) without addressing incentives for health-care providers. My wife, a retinal surgeon, has developed a promising treatment that could save tens of thousands of macular degeneration patients a lifetime of uncomfortable and costly injections and save Medicare at least a billion dollars. Yet there is little financial incentive for the medical world to pursue further development of this treatment, and it will certainly be opposed by drug companies.

3. Government-set standards discourage innovation—the market-place provides it. For several years, various policy makers have tried to impose design standards on technology—which fortunately our industry has defeated, to the benefit everyone. We beat back efforts to restrict recording capability, to add government-mandated buttons to the remote control, to equalize volume, to make every product include features that few would want but all would pay for, and to create products that reject every type of interference. Instead, the industry let the consumers choose what they wanted, and this has produced a robust competitive market that did not foreclose introduction of products like the iPod, the PVR, and HDTV.

Lesson for policy makers: Forcing doctors to follow specific treatment regimens because they save money may dramatically discourage the type of innovation that has made our nation the health-care destination for the world's wealthiest people. However, doctors should be discouraged from excessive testing by measuring the use of reimbursable tests on doctor-owned equipment and restricting physician liability for not conducting marginally valuable tests.

4. Never go large-scale without testing and proving the concept or model first. No company starts without a prototype. The prototype is tested, researched, and given to carefully chosen users for feedback. Nothing is perfect from the start. It takes time and effort. You need to build market demand, raise production, and listen to the feedback.

Lesson for policy makers: Without a national consensus, radically changing by legislative fiat an industry that consumes 17 percent of GDP is a risk that no rational or strategic business would undertake. Congress should roll back the health-care law and try some pilot projects to evaluate their success.

5. When things are not going well, define the real problem. Companies with declining sales undertake rigorous analysis on what they are doing wrong. It's a matter of survival and necessity. When Best Buy was financially challenged over a dozen years ago, it brought in teams that honestly assessed the cause of the problems, and the company changed to correct them and succeed. Companies like Apple, Intel, Motorola, and HP have redefined themselves repeatedly by confronting their problems and acting to shift the direction of the company.

Lesson for Congress: Our nation's health-care costs and large uninsured population are the problems Congress should define and address. The costs stem from a lack of information and com-petition, an obese population (which reportedly adds $147 bil-lion annually to health-care costs), unnecessary legal fees to avoid litigation, and end-of-life treatment. Take together, this consumes almost half of all health-care spending. My father-in-law, a cardi-ologist, performed two invasive cardio procedures recently on two terminal Alzheimer patients who were over ninety years old. The patients lacked living wills, and their family members asked that they be kept alive at any cost. Simply encouraging living wills when getting a drivers license could cut health-care costs.

The health-care debate was important but deceptive and sadly divisive. Like a nation going to war, a consensus was needed, and we never had that consensus. The Obama Administration and the Democrats were never clear on what their core objectives were: was it insuring the uninsured or lowering costs? But rather than attack the problem in a piecemeal way, our government thought it could function in the role of the free market. We will be living with the consequences for some time to come.

Congress should borrow a prescription from the most innovative industries and follow market-driven principles. It should acknowledge that innovations from folks like Jim Traficant are the real cost-reducing tools. Perhaps if we put one hundred government-paid scientists in a room they would eventually have landed upon Jim's idea. But Jim did it without taxpayer dollars.

Above all, government should also remember the physicians' adage: First, do no harm.

Conclusion

KATHY GORNIK AND her college friend, Jim Thiel, had an idea for a better loudspeaker. In 1976 they cobbled together a prototype, packed four days worth of sandwiches, and drove to Chicago for the International Consumer Electronics Show. They exhibited their prototype in a small hotel room and got enough interested retailers to place orders that they could go to a bank and get financing to start manufacturing. Today, Thiel Audio sells speakers throughout the world, and the Thiel factory in Lexington, Kentucky, employs dozens of Americans, knowing that their innovation, craftsmanship, quality, and love of product are enhancing people's lives and contributing to a better world. Kathy is passionate about entrepreneurship, innovation, free markets, capitalism, freedom, and the U.S. Constitution—and the better world they create.

Around the same time Kathy and Jim started Thiel Audio, Loyd Ivey had an idea for better stereo sound. Bored with high school, he dropped out at sixteen, took his ideas and passion for music, and started his sojourn toward producing a better product. He also used CES as a platform to build his business, which became Mitek Corporation, a multi-national audio and electronics company. He has thousands of people employed in the United States and abroad, both imports and exports, and is a huge advocate of free and fair global trade agreements. Loyd's battle cry is "make trade, not war," and he believes in the number one rule that you do not shoot your customers.

Darrell Issa, the son of Christian Lebanese-Arab immigrants, served in the military and, upon returning from deployment, had an idea for a new type of car security system. He created the system, patented the technology, and now millions of cars around the world are empowered with Darrell's voice commanding potential intruders to "get away from the car." Along with his wife, Kathy, Darrell built up his company and sold it for over $100 million. Darrell now serves the public as a member of Congress who understands that businesses, not government, create jobs. This patent owner now chairs the Congressional Committee charged with overseeing efficiency and accountability in government.

John Shalam, an Egyptian-born Jew, escaped the tide of anti-Semitism in Alexandria in 1948 and came to the United States to start a new life. He began a company focused on the fledgling car stereo market and built it into the publically traded powerhouse Audiovox. Today that company is a leader in mobile and consumer electronics and owns many well-known brands such as RCA, Jensen, and Acoustic Research. John is an avid supporter of free trade, free markets, and American innovation. He remains chairman of Audiovox, where he continues to guide the company in its evolution into new markets, new products, and new ventures.

The first-generation son of Chinese immigrants, Noel Lee was a rocket scientist at Lawrence-Livermore. But he quit this safe job to start a band, which left him penniless and playing before senior-citizen groups in Hawaii. He moved back in with his California parents and had an idea for premium wires to connect products. Thus Monster Cable was born, and Noel became its "Head Monster." Despite a disability, he uses his Segway to move him around the world.

Randy Fry, his two brothers, and a friend had an idea for a different type of retailer—one for geeks. They created Fry's Electronics, a huge store in Silicon Valley. The model grew, and they now have thirty-four stores in nine states. Their business model focuses on product selection, service, and merchandising.

Dr. Levy Gerzberg grew up in Israel and received a PhD from Stanford University. He started Zoran Corporation, a California-based, NASDAQ-traded semiconductor company that provides consumer electronics products globally. Dr. Gerzberg's vision was to migrate expensive high-end technology to more affordable system-on-a-chip products, thus bringing the power of high-end technology to consumers. Zoran, under his leadership, developed the camera processor used in the first commercial digital cameras, and Zoran has delivered many innovative, first-to-market technologies for cameras, DVD players, televisions, printers, and other devices.

Blake Krikorian and his brother, grandsons of Armenian immigrants, had an idea for accessing subscription and free television service while away from home. They created Slingbox, and it became a sensation. They sold the company to EchoStar and now spend their time as investors. Blake is passionate about continuing America's innovation advantage.

Bill Crutchfield proved that it doesn't take a government mandate to do good for the environment, and that innovation is not just about products but about doing it better for customers. Each week, Crutchfield's workers in Charlottesville, Virginia, ship thousands of car and home electronics products to customers. Bill started hearing from his customers that they were concerned that the styrofoam packing peanuts used in shipping to protect the products were adding to landfills. Bill sought out alternatives and discovered that cornstarch could be solidified into a type of packaging material using slight modifications to a machine originally designed to make cereal. Moreover, by making the cornstarch peanuts at his facility, he saved several truckloads a month that had been delivering the old-style styrofoam peanuts. Visiting Bill's facility in 2008, I was delighted to see the cornstarch blower and enjoyed eating a few of these "peanuts" hot from the blower. The innovation was good for business and good for the environment.

CAN WE ADD TO THIS LIST?

This list of great American innovators can be much longer. I simply chose a few present or former CEA volunteer leaders to highlight a point. They all had an idea. They put their heart and soul into it. They invested what they had, and they succeeded, thanks to the strength of the idea, their execution, and their good fortune to be born in or immigrate to America. They are living the American Dream, and they have created thousands of American jobs—and none got a penny from the government. And they have given back. They contribute to their favorite causes.

If I have not yet convinced you that our nation must make tough decisions and fundamental changes to preserve the American Dream for our children, then I have failed.

The year 2010 has proven to be one of frustration and anger. Americans by the millions have voiced their displeasure with President Obama and the Democrats, who are taking the brunt of the blame for the poor economy. Much of this anger is justified. The Obama Administration made huge promises and created expectations that could not be met. More, this administration and Congress have helped make the long-term prospects for jobs and growth worse by vastly expanding the deficit, raising payroll taxes, enacting pro-union legislation, fostering protectionism, and creating massive new bureaucracies for health care. The only jobs added have been government jobs, and these jobs simply take money from productive taxpayers to fund non-productive government bureaucracies.

This administration and Congress have also hindered job growth by demonizing businesses and threatening new higher taxes on corporations. The anti-business climate and threats alone were enough to create massive uncertainty in the markets, as investors feared the direction of government and the likelihood of new taxes.

In addition to this parade of horrors, the job-challenged U.S. economy has huge structural issues that the Obama Administration did not cause—although it may have exacerbated them. We have lost millions of jobs due to an economy that was fueled by sub-prime mortgages. We are now considered, for the first time in our lifetimes, a less attractive slow-growth environment for investment compared to many other countries. We are beginning to wonder if the new unemployment "normal" will be defined as in the high single-digits. This number, of course, excludes an almost equal number of discouraged or under-employed workers.

The challenge we face is not that we need more government programs to create jobs. We need government to get out of the way and allow new businesses to be created, new investment to occur, and innovation to be unleashed. That is what much of this book is about: a framework for competitiveness and innovation.

But today Congress is incapable of addressing the fundamental challenges raised in this book. It is simply impossible in the present environment for Congress to pass legislation focusing on the fundamental problems facing America's future. Instead, each congressional committee jealously guards its prerogatives and has little desire to be part of any national solutions on innovation or competitiveness. For example, trade legislation is handled in the House by the Ways and Means Committee, immigration is handled by the Judiciary Committee, and government spending by Appropriations and Budget Committees.

To formulate a national strategy addressing our present crisis, one possible solution is for Congress to act with comprehensive legislation, which can be referred to for action by various committees. This was done after 9/11, when several committees contributed to the Patriot Act and the creation of the Homeland Security legislation.

Another approach, would be for the House to create a new committee with broad responsibility for innovation and competitiveness. It would have jurisdiction over many of the issues discussed in this book, including trade, immigration, and investment. If given a mandate to enact serious reform (and if appropriately staffed by responsible lawmakers who were concerned about our children's future rather than today's entitlements), it would be possible to find a national solution. Indeed, today the House acts with several committees of experts. Every member has expertise in a certain area, and when bipartisan legislation emerges (which it actually often does), other members defer to the committee composed of experts.

But what we first need is a national debate on priorities. This has not occurred. The debate today is over jobs. Democrats argue for more government spending and programs. Republicans argue for lower taxes. While the Democratic programs provide short-term jobs in government, they create larger deficits, which steal from tomorrow to pay for today. And while lowering taxes will produce economic growth and jobs, that, too, will increase the deficit. The challenge is for government to focus on the long-term deficit and to create a current economic environment favoring job creation and growth. This requires the type of priority-setting described throughout this book.

We are in a crisis, and it won't be fixed simply by more government spending or by cutting taxes. Our growing sense of entitlement is destroying America's innovative culture, which is the true engine of economic growth.

In Britain, new Prime Minister David Cameron came into office in early 2010 with a mandate to change the country, which was struggling under a mountain of debt and poor economic growth. Worse, public services were beginning to break down. In a matter of months, Cameron radically cut entitlement programs and government spending while selectively raising taxes, and he successfully put the British back on a course to fiscal sanity.

Cameron's success shows that a country can come back from the edge if its leaders are willing to make hard decisions and be straight with the public (and themselves). Even though our democracy works a bit differently than the British, real reform is possible. But it requires action. And if our political leaders can't yet muster the courage to act, then perhaps we need to give them a nudge.

If you are still with me, you can do something. CEA is advocating many of the positions in this book through its Innovation Movement. This grassroots effort is designed to develop a cadre of Americans committed to the future of their children and of their country. It believes our prosperity will come through entrepreneurship, innovation, and free market principles. It does not advocate additional government spending!

You can sign up for this growing movement at www.innovation-movement.com.

Together, we can send the message to Washington that greater prosperity requires innovation. It does not require more government. Government at its best will be neutral. At its worst, it will get in the way and create barriers to innovation, investment, trade, and the creation of long-term jobs.

Innovation *is* America. It is our special sauce, our destiny, and our best and only hope for escaping the economic malaise, which decades of excessive government spending and intrusion have created. Our best hope is for government to foster innovation by creating a fertile ground for innovation to flourish.

Innovation is a natural by-product of the free market. It is not the result of government coercion. You can't legislate progress. You can't will an iPad into existence with committee hearings and tax dollars. It is the innovators' job to fill a need, whether urgent or unknown, better than an existing competitor. Innovation has winners and losers, and the losers must be allowed to exit quickly so that other entrants can enter the game.

Our nation is looking into the abyss. With a blinding focus on the present, our government is neglecting a future that demands thoughtful action. The only valid government action is that which invests in our children. This requires hard choices. We cannot leave the rising generation with a mountain of bad debt. This will require suffering in the present. We need to cut entitlements, cut government programs, pull back from being the world's policeman, and reform our "sue everybody" culture. If we act with a plan that values free market innovation, our children have a chance for a better life.

In 2008, I gave a speech at Wayne State University, right outside Detroit. I addressed it to my unborn son. It read, in part:

Dear Son,

If all goes according to plan, in a few weeks you will be born at Beaumont Hospital. You enter the world at a historic time. It is a time of uncertainty, politically, financially, and internationally. But the history that your children, grandchildren, and their progeny will study about this era will not be about politics or about conflicts; it will be about a fundamental and seismic change in technology.

My great-grandparents talked about the early 1900s being a big shift in the world. They described how they entered a world of huge distances—covered by slow ships at sea and the horse-and-buggy on land. But when they were teenagers, at the turn of the last century, we moved to the smaller world of the car and the airplane. These technologies began the century where our people, our nation, and our world changed. New industries formed. Our possibilities expanded. Our standard of living rose.

But the revolution coinciding with your birth is even bigger. The shift to digital technology is still in its infancy, but the next year marks a huge milestone. It started with big computers and the compact disc in the 1980s. Then PCs, DVDs, and cellular phones became popular in the 1990s. Now we have digital cameras, BluRay, and high-definition televisions.

It's probably fair to say that you wouldn't be here without digital TV. I first met your mom when I was sitting next to her on a chair lift and she was talking about HDTV on her cell phone. Even though I knew everything about HDTV, I played innocent and I asked her what HDTV was. She explained it so perfectly that I immediately was enchanted with her. The rest is history.

So, you are a HDTV baby, and you are entering a world that will soon be entirely digital. It is your destiny to live during the digital revolution and to live a very different life than your father.

When I was born, there were only a few consumer electronics products. We had radio and black-and-white TV. That was basically it. Indeed, back then, the Consumer Electronics Association was called the Radio and Television Manufacturers Association. We only had one choice of telephone—a black rotary phone. Lucky families had a phonograph player. Wealthier families bought 16-millimeter cameras.

But we have come a long way. Today, the average American home owns twenty-five consumer electronics products and spends some $1,500 on products and another $1,000 on services each year.

The average family now owns 2.77 television sets. Music is portable, and almost everyone has at least one MP3 player. Just about every family has a digital camera. The manual typewriter is a historic relic, and 75 percent of American homes have a computer. It is estimated that smartphone sales will surpass PC sales this year.

With competition between cable, telephone, fiber, and other services, 65 percent of Americans have broadband at home—and even more have it at their office. This alone has encouraged new businesses and services. Think of all the great American companies that rely on computers and the Internet: Amazon, eBay, Google, Yahoo, and thousands of cool new services have been created thanks to this explosion in technology.

It has been a wonderful shift to digital. Digital is our destiny. It has been my privilege to play a role in digital television, to lead the charge promoting innovation, and to lead the international Consumer Electronics Show. The CES, held each January in Las Vegas, is the world's coolest technology event and America's largest event of any type. Over 2,500 companies introduce some 20,000 products at each show, and the event attracts everyone interested in the digital revolution.

But the shift to digital is just the beginning. What about the future? What about the next twenty years?

I am passionate about innovation because I believe it will create new opportunities and will solve many challenges we now face. But our digital destiny is not divinely set in stone. It depends on the government allowing the free market to find its way. It depends on rewarding innovation, not punishing successful businesses. It means the government must ensure free trade so innovative products and capital and investment can find their natural level. It means ignoring the pleas of old industries for protection. We didn't protect the horse-and-buggy makers when the car came along. We didn't protect travel agents with the advent of the Internet. And we shouldn't protect any industry hurt by innovation that pleads its case for government intervention. The free market can hurt. Companies and even entire industries can topple. But that's progress.

So to you, my unborn son, I say you are lucky to be joining this world at such an exciting time. It will be trying and joyful. It will be fast-paced. It will be different.

We are at the end of the beginning of the digital revolution, and it is almost all good. Our future is bright. Our nation is poised to lead. You will be a torchbearer for this new world of opportunity, enlightenment, and prosperity. I wish you Godspeed and good luck, and I will be there as long as I can, as the old fogey who doesn't understand the new technology.

Today, I might write a different letter. Although we remain in exciting times, the future doesn't look as bright as it did on that day at Wayne State. America is in crisis. What is required is a commitment to innovation and growth. We can and must succeed. With popular and political resolve, we can reverse America's decline. My goal is simple: Americans must become the world's innovative engine once again; we cannot fail. Only then can I return to China and tell that Communist Chinese official that America is back.

Acknowledgments

A BOOK, I have learned, is not the same thing as a speech or column or a combination of both. It is an enterprise requiring an army. And while the initial writing is a solitary experience requiring often painful exercises in transforming ideas and vignettes into sensible prose and order, a final publishable product involves many people pushing in the same direction.

First, I thank my wife, Dr. Susan Malinowski, for her humor, brilliance, empathy, and love. She has always encouraged me, served as a sounding board, and found time for me despite being a mother, full-time doctor, entrepreneur, patent owner, innovator in surgical techniques, and writer. Her parents, Drs. Edward and Jolanta Malinowski, have never stopped making the world better by selflessly giving to others, and have generously given their time, allowing me to write this book.

I thank my parents, Jerome and Mildred Shapiro, for somehow instilling in me and my three brothers, Eric, Ken and Howie, the ability to think outside the box and the confidence to believe we can do things better. The gift of confidence is one of the most important a parent can bestow.

I thank my children, Steve and Doug, for keeping me humble, giving me joy, and each becoming fine adults. I thank and acknowledge their mother and my former wife, Jan Wolf, for doing so much to raise them to be ethical and educated at the same time she supported my desire to further my career.

I thank the CEA Executive Board. Rarely are association boards so strategic on so many levels. Its focus with and concern about the long-term health of the U.S. economy gave me the voice to express the ideas in this book. Their willingness to entrust me and the CEA staff on the execution of many of these ideas has made CEA an effective agent for positive change. I am so grateful they encouraged me on this book and my other writings. Thank you to Gary Yacoubian, Randy Fry, Pat Lavelle, John Godfrey, Mark Luden, Denise Gibson, Ian Hendler, Jim Bazet, Brian Dunn, Stan Glasgow, Loyd Ivey, Jay McLellan, Peter Lesser, Peter Fannon, Noel Lee, Steve Caldero, Paul Sabbah, Grant Russell, and Mike Mohr.

I thank many of our former leaders who have taught me so much: Joe Clayton, who taught me about passion (and results: "once is a blip and twice is a trend"); Jerry Kalov, who molded me into an executive and told me he would stand by me when I failed (and I often did); Eddie Hartenstein, who demonstrated emotional intelligence (and literally picked me up in the rain when I needed a ride to emcee a dinner); John Shalam, whose sheer goodness is an inspiration; Kathy Gornik, who loves liberty; Bill Crutchfield, who often engaged me on politics and business and helped refine my thoughts; and Congressman Darrell Issa, who chaired our board, ran a business, owns patents, and is the model of what every American should contribute to the national debate.

I thank CEA executive Jason Oxman, who heard my dream of writing a book, encouraged me, and helped me take what I thought was a near-final draft and push it much further to make it a real book. I also thank many on his team, such as Laurie Ann Phillips and Megan Pollock, who read early drafts and gave comments. I am grateful to our policy head Michael Petricone for giving me his guidance and trying to save me from unfairly dishing dirt.

I appreciate our Research Center and market research staff for gathering the facts and data that underlies the book. I thank our tech team, headed by Brian Markwalter, for focusing on moving the industry forward and getting the technical issues that support innovation right. I thank our show team, headed by Karen Chupka, for producing the world's most glorious event, the International CES, and making sure our industry gets the world's attention. I thank our CFO, Glenda MacMullin, for running our operations, and lawyer John Kelly for helping guide us in a reasonable and fair way of publishing the book. I also thank the entire CEA staff for always plugging for me, our members, and the innovation industry. Their enthusiasm, hard work, and love for innovation make me look forward to coming to work every day.

I thank my assistant, Jana Sievers, for always going the extra yard, never complaining about my handwriting, and delivering new drafts while also managing scores of other projects. A special call out to the first person who worked with me on the book, our intern, Karie Palmer, who helped me edit early drafts and coordinated my travel during a difficult time.

I also thank various people for their reviews and comments: David Leibowitz, Bob Schwartz, Julie Kearney, and Veronica O'Connell. I appreciate the patient care of Katie Hallen and Tom Galvin and their colleagues at the 463 Group for their ideas and edits to earlier speeches and columns, and their work on the Innovation Movement, which helped inspire this book.

I acknowledge Dick Wiley, John Taylor, Joe Flaherty, Mark Richer (another MacArthur grad), Robert Graves, David Donovan, Peter Fannon, and Bryan Burns for their unwavering commitment to HDTV.

I thank all my colleagues who head other technology groups, including CCIA, CTIA, ITI, JEDEC, NVTC, SIA, SIIA, TIA, TechAmerica,

TechNet, and the Technology CEO Council. Each contributes to moving innovation forward.

I especially appreciate the work of my editor, Blake D. Dvorak. His sheer competence allowed me to accept the many changes, edits, and cuts to syntax, sentences, and even ideas I loved and thought were perfect. He improved this book in ways I couldn't imagine and has been the first in a while to have the unique combination of courage, confidence, and charisma to cow me into accepting edits. I also acknowledge the Pinkston Group, especially Christian Pinkston and David Fouse, for helping the book idea come to fruition.

I thank Beaufort Books for working with me on this book on many levels: the flexibility you showed and the patience and willingness to take risks reflect well on our theme of innovation. Any mistakes are mine, and do not necessarily reflect the positions of the publisher or the Consumer Electronics Association.

I want to thank the lawyers at Squire Sanders, who tore up my early writing and taught me how to write. I appreciate my background in law from Georgetown University Law School and my economics training from Binghamton University. A special shout out to my experience at MacArthur High School; seeing the early Richard Viguerie's conservative rants on the walls taught me that freedom of expression is a gift not to be wasted. My decade-plus of 4-H also inspired me to be ethical and contribute to society.

I also acknowledge Grover Norquist for his principled leadership, and Ed Meese and Dr. Alan Merten for teaching me so much through their leadership when I served on the George Mason University Board. I thank Gigi Sohn and the Public Knowledge team, CATO, Competitive Enterprise Institute, the Peter G. Peterson Foundation, and Third Way, who all inspired portions of the thinking in this book.

I also want to acknowledge Mark Penn and his wife Nancy Jacobsen. Nancy began the No Labels movement, composed of real

Americans focused on policy for the nation rather than politics by party line. She, along with the No Labels group of thinkers, have bolstered my view that our nation is in trouble and neither party is providing solutions.

I acknowledge some great business leaders who have inspired me: Ivan Seidenberg of Verizon not only received CEA's highest award and leads a phenomenal company, he was also the first corporation head to stand up in 2010 and declare that our government is hurting business and job creation. John Chambers of Cisco, Craig Barrett and Paul Ottellini of Intel, Alan Mulally of Ford, Brian Roberts of Comcast, the Hubbards of Hubbard Broadcasting, Bill Gates and Steve Balmer of Microsoft, Jeff Bezos of Amazon, and every top leader of Best Buy have all had a big vision that transcended the typical corporate focus on the next quarter. They are strategic, innovation-focused, and passionate about the future of our country.

I also have to recognize a few political leaders whose integrity gives me hope. Former Congressman Rick Boucher raises the average IQ of every room he enters and approached legislation with a bias towards innovation, a willingness to engage in details, and an open mind. Congressman Gregory Meeks is willing to fight the standard anti–free trade message of his party. Congressman Joe Barton stands up for the rule of law and process and facts. Fred Upton, Cliff Stearns, Marsha Blackburn, and Lee Terry each are principled Congressmen who focus on facts and favor the free market and entrepreneurship. Congressman Paul Ryan has singularly raised the big uncomfortable issues. Senator Tom Coburn insists on good legislation in the Senate and uses his power to force it. Senator Mark Warner understands innovation, and Governors Mitt Romney, Tim Pawlenty, Chris Christie, and Mitch Daniels inspire me, show promise, can make tough choices, and are willing to deviate from their party line. New York City Mayor Michael Bloomberg thinks outside the box and would also be a wonderful presidential candidate. Every one of these Americans does what's right, and political contributions have no impact on their views.

Finally, I thank the American people. Together we share this moment in time, and together we will succeed or fail. I hope this book inspires you to join the cause of innovation and embrace it as our gift to the next generation.

Bibliography

Acs, Zoltan and Laszlo Szerb. "Global Entrepreneurship and the United States." Small Business Association. September 2010.

Allen, Mike and Jonathan Weisman. "Steel Tariffs Appeared to Have Backfired on Bush: Move to Aid Mills and Gain Votes in 2 States Is Called Political and Economic Mistake." *Washington Post.* September 19, 2003. http://www.washingtonpost.com/ac2/wp-dyn?pagename=article&node=&contentId=A31768-2003Sep18.

American College of Surgeons. "Statement from the American College of Surgeons Regarding Recent Comments from President Obama." August 12, 2009. http://www.facs.org/news/obama081209.html.

American Tort Reform Association. "Tort Reform Record: June 2010." http://www.atra.org.

Argitis, Theophilos. "Canada Lawmakers Ratify Free Trade Agreement With Colombia, Send to Senate." *Bloomberg.* June 14, 2010. http://www.businessweek.com/ news/2010-06-14/canadian-lawmakers-approve-free-trade-agreement-with-colombia.html.

Bender, Joshua, et al. "An Education Strategy to Promote Opportunity, Prosperity, and Growth." The Bookings Institution. February 2007.

Bergsten, C. Fred. "How Best to Boost U.S. Exports." *Washington Post.* February 3, 2010. http://www.washingtonpost.com/wp-dyn/content/article/2010/02/02/AR2010020203301.html.

Berners-Lee, Tim. "Frequently Asked Questions." *w3.*http://www.w3.org/People/Berners-Lee/FAQ.html.

Brill, Steven. "The Rubber Room." *The New Yorker.* August 31, 2009.

Brown, Angela. "Flint Number 3 in U.S. for Population Loss." *ABC News 12, WJRT.* June 22, 2010. http://abclocal.go.com/wjrt/story?section=news/local&id=7512972.

Burrelli, Joan. "Foreign Science and Engineering Students in the United States." National Science Foundation. July 2010. http://www.nsf.gov/statistics/infbrief/nsf10324.

"CBO report: Debt Will Rise to 90% of GDP." *Washington Times.* March 26, 2010.

Chao, Loretta. "China Issued Record Number of Patents in 2009." *The Wall Street Journal.* February 4, 2010. http://online.wsj.com/article/sb10014240527487035 75004575042691331624302.html.

"Colombia Consumer Electronics Report." *Snipsly.* June 22, 2010. http://snipsly. com/2010/06/22/colombia-consumer-electronics-report.

Congressional Budget Office. "Discretionary Spending in the Final Health Care Legislation." May 11, 2010. http://cboblog.cbo.gov/?p=835.

Crowe, Darcy. "Colombia: Exports To Reach $40 Billion in '10; Double in 4 Years." *The Wall Street Journal.* September 8, 2010. http://online.wsj.com/article/BT-CO-20100908-713536.html.

Dalton, Matthew and John W. Miller. "EU Nations Approve Free Trade Pact With South Korea." *The Wall Street Journal.* September 17, 2010. http://online.wsj. com/article/SB10001424052748703440604575495201694209806 .html?mod=googlenews_wsj.

Davis, Teddy, Jennifer Parker, and Kate Snow. "Obama Campaign Denies Duplicity On Trade." ABC. March 3, 2008. http://abcnews.go.com/Politics/DemocraticDebate/story?id=4380122&page=1.

Ebeling, Richard M. "Obama Thanks His Friends: Government Spending and Union Support." American Institute for Economic Research. June 8, 2009. http:// www.aier.org/research/briefs/1550-obama-thanks-his-friends-government-spending-and-union-support.

"FASB's Tort Bar Gift." *The Wall Street Journal.* August 18, 2010. http://online.wsj .com/article/SB10001424052748704554104575435851610547946.html.

Gentry, William M. and R. Glenn Hubbard. "Success Taxes, Entrepreneurial Entry, and Innovation." *Social Science Research Network.* June 2004. http://papers. ssrn.com/sol3/papers.cfm?abstract_id=556538.

Goldman, Julianna and Nicholas Johnston. "Obama Turns Focus to Trade as Way to Encourage Economic Growth." *Bloomberg.* September 16, 2010. http://www .bloomberg.com/news/2010-09-16/obama-turns-focus-to-trade-as-way-to-encourage-economic-growth.html.

Haltiwanger, John C., Ron S. Jarmin, Javier Miranda. National Bureau of Economic Research. Working Paper 16300. August 2010.

Henig, Robin Marantz. "What Is It About 20-Somethings?: Why are so many people in their 20s taking so long to grow up?" *New York Times.* August 18, 2010. http://www. nytimes.com/2010/08/22/magazine/22Adulthood-t.html?_r=2&pagewanted=all.

Hindman, Nathaniel Cahners. "Innovation Shifted To China During The Downturn: U.N. Report." *Huffington Post.* September 16, 2010. http://www .huffingtonpost.com/2010/09/16/innovation-shifted-to-chi_n_718363.html.

"Intuit 2020 Report 'Twenty Trends That Will Shape The Next Decade'." *Intuit.* October 2010. http://about.intuit.com/futureofsmallbusiness.

Jorde, Thomas M. and David J. Teece. "Innovation, Dynamic, Competition, and Antitrust Policy," Cato Institute. 1990.

Kane, Tim. "The Importance of Startups in Job Creation and Job Destruction." The Kauffman Foundation. July 2010. http://www.kauffman.org/uploadedFiles/firm_formation_importance_of_startups.pdf.

Konrad, Rachel. "Immigrants behind 25 Percent of Tech Startups." *MSNBC.* January 3, 2007. http://www.msnbc.msn.com/id/16459952.

"Labor: Long-Term Contribution Trends." *Opensecrets*. Center for Responsive Politics. October 25, 2010.

Levy, Francesca. "America's 25 Richest Counties." *Forbes*. March 4, 2010. http://www .forbes.com/2010/03/04/america-richest-counties-lifestyle-real-estate-wealthy-suburbs.html.

Levy, Robert A. "Do's and Don'ts of Tort Reform." CATO Institute. May 2005. http:// www.cato.org/pub_display.php?pub_id=4566.

Malseed, Mark. "The Story of Sergey Brin: How the Moscow-born entrepreneur cofounded Google and changed the way the world searches." *Moment*. February 2007. http://www.momentmag.com/Exclusive/2007/2007-02/200702-BrinFeature. html.

Matsuura, Jeffrey H. "Thomas Jefferson and the Evolution of a Populist Vision of Intellectual Property Rights and Democratic Values." *Archipelago*. November 3, 2006. http://www.archipelago.org/vol10-34/matsuura.htm.

Muller, Joann. "Ford Is Slowly Climbing Out Of Debt." *Forbes*. July 23, 2010. http://www.forbes.com/2010/07/23/autos-ford-debt-business-autos-ford-debt.html.

Murray, Sara. "City Unemployment: Vegas, Washington at Opposite Ends." *The Wall Street Journal*. July 28, 2010. http://blogs.wsj.com/economics/2010/07/28/city-unemployment-rates-for-june-vegas-worst-washington-best.

"Obama: The American combat mission in Iraq has ended." *CNN*. August 31, 2010. http://politicalticker.blogs.cnn.com/2010/08/31/obama-the-american-combat-mission-in-iraq-has-ended.

Organisation for Economic Co-Operation and Development. "OECD Broadband Portal." June 10, 2010. http://www.oecd.org/document/54/0,3343,en_2649_34 225_38690102_1_1_1_1,00.html.

Palmer, Doug. "G20 Summit Could Give Doha Talks a Lift: WTO's Lamy." *ABC News*. September 22, 2010. http://abcnews.go.com/Business/wireStory?id=11702102.

Pawlenty, Tim. "Time for Obama to make sacrifices." *Politico*. July 14, 2010. http:// www.politico.com/news/stories/0710/39674.html.

Rockefeller, Edwin S. "Time for Anitrust to Bite the Dust." *The Wall Street Journal*. August 19, 2010. http://online.wsj.com/article/SB100014240527487048686045 75433750492881746.html.

Rosenburg, Nathan. "Innovation and Economic Growth." Stanford University. 2004. http://www.oecd.org/dataoecd/55/49/34267902.pdf .

Schneider, Howard. "Obama's ambitious export plan may rekindle free-trade battle." *Washington Post*. March 12, 2010. http://www.washingtonpost.com/wp-dyn/ content/article/2010/03/11/AR2010031100739.html.

Schultz, George, et al. "Principles for Economic Revival." *The Wall Street Journal*. September 16, 2010.

Sinai, Allen. "Cap Gains Taxation: Less Means More." *The Wall Street Journal*. September 21, 2010. http://online.wsj.com/article/ SB10001424052748703556 604575501892210065882.html.

United States. Office of the United States Intellectual Property Enforcement Coordinator. *Intellectual Property Spotlight*. August 2010. http://www. whitehouse.gov/sites/default/files/omb/assets/intellectualproperty/IPEC_ Spotlight_August2010.pdf.

United States. Office of the Vice President. "Summer of Recovery: Project Activity Increases in Summer." June 17, 2010. http://www.whitehouse.gov/sites/default/files/RecoverySummer_Report.pdf.

United States. U.S. Chamber of Commerce. *Opening Markets, Creating Jobs: Estimated U.S. Employment Effects of Trade with FTA Partners.* 2010. http://www.uschamber.com/sites/default/files/reports/100514_ftajobs_full_0.pdf.

United States. U.S. Chamber of Commerce. *Trade Action—or Inaction: The Cost for American Workers and Companies.* September 15, 2009. http://www.uschamber.com/sites/default/files/reports/uscc_trade_action_inaction_study.pdf.

United States. U.S. Department of Education. "A Nation at Risk." April 1983. http://www2.ed.gov/pubs/NatAtRisk/risk.html.

United States. U.S. Department of Education. *Highlights from PISA 2006: Performance of U.S. 15-Year-Old Students in Science and Mathematics Literacy in an International Context.* December 2007. http://nces.ed.gov/pubs2008/2008016.pdf.

United States. U.S. Patent and Trademark Office. *Patenting by Organizations 2008.* December 2008. http://www.uspto.gov/web/offices/ac/ido/oeip/taf/ topo_08.htm#ToD.

Wadhwa, Vivek. "Foreign-Born Entrepreneur: An Underestimated American Resource." *Kauffman Thoughtbook. 2009.* 177–181. http://www.kauffman.org/uploadedFiles/WadhwaTBook09.pdf.

Whitman, Meg. "California Pension Reform." *National Review Online.* April 23, 2010. http://www.nationalreview.com/articles/229617/california-pension-reform/meg-whitman.

Will, George. "Not a State-Broken People." *Real Clear Politics.* July 26, 2010. http://www.realclearpolitics.com/articles/2010/07/26/not_a_state-broken_people_106463.html.

Williams, Corey. "Detroit Fires Add to Burned, Vacant Landscape." *ABC News.* September 9, 2010. http://abcnews.go.com/US/wireStory?id=11588645.

Williamson, Elizabeth. "Obama Shifts to Export-Led Jobs Push." *The Wall Street Journal.* July 7, 2010. http://online.wsj.com/article/SB1000142405274870363640457535273125819629 8.html.

Williamson, Kevin. "The Other National Debt." *National Review Online.* June 14, 2010. http://www.nationalreview.com/articles/229942/other-national-debt/kevin-williamson?page=1.

Zahniser, David. "Two L.A. agencies get $111 million in stimulus funds but have created only 55 jobs." *Los Angeles Times.* September 17, 2010. http://www.latimes.com/news/local/la-me-stimulus-audit-20100917,0,3706864.story.